What people are saying about
Bipolar Disorder—Insights for Recovery

"Dr. Mountain has personally triumphed over bipolar depression, and I have been fortunate to watch her transformation. She has a unique insight into this disorder—that of a physician, an advocate and an individual with bipolar disorder. This book will be important to people with bipolar disorders and their families." *Robyn Loup, Board Member, Mental Health Association of Colorado and National Mental Health Association.*

"Dr. Mountain is a knowledgeable professional in the field of Mental Health and shares her knowledge with others in words that a layperson can understand." *Al Rue, President of the North City Park Civic Association of Denver.*

More of what people are saying about
Bipolar Disorder—Insights for Recovery

"IN *BIPOLAR DISORDER—Insights for Recovery* Dr. Mountain applies her medical expertise to accurately describe bipolar disorder and the recovery process. She speaks with a powerful combination of compassion and understanding. The book is especially compelling for those with bipolar disorder." *Claire M. Ohman, PhD, Chemist, President of the Board, Mental Health Ombuds Program of Colorado.*

"AS ONE WHO has lived with bipolar disorder, I have had several opportunities to hear Jane Mountain speak at my recovery group. I have always found her information enlightening, her insights helpful and her personal journey encouraging. Jane speaks from her personal experience, her observations, her medical training and her caring heart. Family members and individuals with bipolar disorder will benefit from this book." *Richard Dalton, an individual with bipolar disorder.*

To Chuck, my husband and life mate.
You help calm my restless spirit.

« How beautiful upon the mountains
are the feet of him who brings peace. »

From Nahum 1.15

Bipolar Disorder
Insights for Recovery

Jane Mountain MD

Chapter One Press

Bipolar Disorder—Insights for Recovery
by Jane Mountain MD

www.beyondbipolar.com

This book is not meant to substitute for medical care of people with bipolar disorder, and treatment should not be based solely on its contents. Nor is it meant to offer legal advice, which must be obtained from a practicing attorney.

Chapter One Press

P.O. BOX 300039
Denver, Colorado 80203-0039
Printed in USA

Editing: *Barbara McNichol Editorial*, Phoenix, AZ
Printing: *United Graphics, Inc.*, Mattoon, IL
Cover design & page layout:
Chuck Mountain Graphic Design, Denver, CO

Principal typefaces: Adobe Garamond Pro & Letraset Papyrus
Typesetting: Adobe InDesign 2.0.2 on an Apple PowerPC G4 (OS X)

Contents
Table of Contents

Acknowledgements

Acknowledgements

WRITING AND PUBLISHING a book is a substantial project and the work of many lives. Here are but a few of the people who have contributed to this book—

Chuck, my husband and life-mate of 32 years; our son *Nathan*, gift to our marriage, bringer of joy and my hero; *Alan Shiffrin*, MD, teacher, colleague and healer; *Aunt Donna Cooley*, encourager and keeper of hope through times of trial; *Hue Vo*, MD, friend and confidant; *Claire Ohman*, PHD, and *Dawn Reichert*, friends in time of need and celebration; *members* of the Depression/Bipolar Recovery Group of Midtown Denver; *Jeff Logan*, CHP-PA, and *Nona Yeager*, CNP/COHN, forever my colleagues in healing; *Alice Weiss-Doyel*, encourager and entrepreneur extraordinaire, *Carol Eve Moon*, MD, stretcher of my unreachable goals; *Linda Lange*, financial advisor and unfailing supporter; *Hal Lunka*, PMP, mentor and friend; *Barbara McNichol*, editor. All those who read the original manuscript—*Hal Lunka, Claire Ohman, Lucy Radatz, Alan Shiffrin*, MD, and *Alice Weiss Doyel; Chapter One Press.*

Introduction
The Importance of This Book

THERE IS a need for this book. Whenever I give a workshop, I can see the hunger for insight in the audience members. Their reactions are peppered throughout my presentation, acknowledging my understanding of their daily experience with bipolar disorder. Some laugh. Some nod. Others turn to the person beside them, their eyes silently communicating, "She really does understand. That's how it feels. That's what it's like."

I have given workshops about living with bipolar disorder for more than four years. Almost always, someone asks if I have written a book containing the information and ideas shared in my presentations. If they themselves do not have bipolar disorder, they know of family members and friends who do. They realize that understanding this illness is the first step toward recovering from it. And they want the insights in an easy-reference, sharable form.

They're hungry for this because it enables them to live with an illness that threatens their lives. In chance meetings with audience members months or years later, I learn that something I said sparked a sense of empowerment and gave them hope to live better with the challenges of bipolar disorder.

My passion to understand bipolar disorder is fueled by several of my own life experiences. First and foremost is having this illness myself as well as having a close family member who has it. Like many people in my audiences, I have been overwhelmed by the power of this illness and its ability to rob my life of enjoyment and functionality. I have struggled to regain mental wellness in the face of living with a disorder that nearly destroyed me.

Second, my career as a family physician provides training as well as insight into experiences of both health and illness for individuals and families. In practice as a physician and in life as a patient, my goal has been to consistently combine the art and science of medicine. I have worked hard to take health and illness out of a theoretical context and into the practical, everyday experiences of real people. This is the time—during everyday life—when healing occurs and when wellness emerges from the reluctant womb of illness.

Third, my passion for knowledge has been nurtured by hundreds of individuals with bipolar disorder whom I have met as a mental health speaker, trainer and advocate. Their creativity, courage and resiliency have taught me to draw strength from others who share similar challenges.

Bipolar disorder isn't an experience of individuals but rather of families, communities and society. My teachers have walked the streets of homelessness, sat in the chairs of disability and run the marathons of disenfranchisement. They have also walked the halls of higher education, sat on the couches of creativity and run the races of leadership.

Bipolar disorder doesn't discriminate. It both impoverishes and empowers. Its tentacles reach from the council chambers of presidents and prime ministers to the creative imagination of poets and artists, bringing a special giftedness to accompany its destructive power. Truly, bipolar disorder engenders helplessness and hopelessness, but also generates power and courage.

I have written this book to share insights that have proven helpful to me and hundreds of others. Studies about recovery show that the insights discussed in these chapters make up the first small steps toward managing this illness.

It is, therefore, important to know the facts about bipolar disorder, and I hope all readers continue to learn as much as they can. Many books and resources are available to increase our knowledge. (I have included a list of these in the Recovery Resources section, pp 141-143.)

My goal is to personalize the facts in an easy-reference format that empowers you not just to survive but also to fully enjoy a rewarding life. Believe me, you can continue to seek mental wellness, even in the context of experiencing bipolar disorder. *Bipolar Disorder—Insights for Recovery* tells you how to begin.

Gaining Hope to Manage Bipolar Disorder

B IPOLAR DISORDER causes pain. You are already aware of this or you wouldn't be reading this book. The newly gained insights in *Bipolar Disorder—Insights for Recovery* will help you better manage its impact on your life.

Sometimes when we begin learning on a deeper level about an illness, we ignore its painful side. We can forget that we are, first and foremost, individuals experiencing very real pain. If this describes you, even if you are feeling hopeless, let me remind you—there is an excellent chance you can get better.

The emotional pain of bipolar disorder is completely different from physical pain. For one thing, emotional pain deeply affects relationships with friends and family members. When someone experiences physical pain, you may easily find words to console and encourage that person. But when you suffer the deep emotional pain of bipolar disorder, you likely feel you're not getting support from others. Indeed, to protect yourself, you hide your pain and try to disguise your symptoms.

This doesn't mean that people who do not experience a mental illness do not feel emotional pain. There is not a person living who has not known emotional pain from loss—the loss of a loved one through death or divorce, for example. Even the loss of a beloved family pet can be extremely hard to bear.

But the emotional pain of bipolar disorder has a different quality—and is experienced much more intensely—than these examples. This pain can be so intense that we may not want to live. This pain, coupled with hopelessness, can lead to suicide.

UNRELENTING PAIN

In addition, this pain is unrelenting. The pain of grief, for example, causes people to experience overwhelming sadness, but they still have moments punctuated by other emotions. However, the emotional stress of sadness experienced with bipolar depression or the potentially destructive qualities of mania, can be so overwhelming that other emotions are blotted out. In this state of heart and mind, it is impossible to remember what it felt like not to have this pain. It seems never-ending.

Let me use myself as an example. When I felt this intense pain, I was so overwhelmed that I didn't want to live an hour, a minute or even a second longer. Life felt like a dense atmosphere of swirling gray smog that threatened to suffocate me. If you find yourself in this state, remember: Even if you are feeling this pain, you can get better. I did!

HOPE

In the meantime, you may have to ask others to hope for you. Surround yourself with optimistic people—a doctor or therapist, a family member, a friend or even a pet. Rely on their hope to help you when your ability to hope seems lost.

I once came across a painting titled Hope. The background of the painting is right out of the Apocalypse—war, destruction, disease and death. In the foreground, a little to one side, is a woman in a tattered and frayed white garment. Her name is Hope. Hope holds a small harp in her arms, a harp with every string broken except one. As she plucks that single string, her eyes turn upward, gazing up at the graying sky with the slightest smile on her bright face. Defying circumstances, she plays on.

Right now, this painting may seem absurd. The deep depression of bipolar disorder or the overwhelming influence of mania can make Hope seem ludicrous. Doesn't she see the despair around her? And isn't she tired of playing on that one string? At one time, my depression taunted me to look only at the painting's chaotic background. But Hope wanted me to look beyond despair. I found that single image immensely comforting.

Even though it may not seem possible in your wildest dreams, know that hope exists. This cannot be emphasized enough. Once I went to a workshop and the workshop leader had at one time been seriously ill with bipolar depression. She spoke for three hours, sharing all of the reasons we have to find hope in our lives. I could hardly take it all in! Her message is this: *Don't ever give up.* You, too, can have hope even though your illness tells you otherwise. Look for Hope; she's still there.

LOSSES

In addition to the extreme emotional pain of depression, you may also experience grief over many other kinds of loss—loss of independence, loss of ability to function, loss of friendships, loss of ability to work and loss of identity. As you learn more about bipolar disorder, you will understand how these losses occur. Then you can explore what you can do to deal with them. If you feel you have lost a part of yourself or a part of your life to bipolar disorder, you are not alone. If you are grieving these losses, you are not alone. These things are commonplace, but they can be overcome and, in many cases, prevented.

THE FLIP SIDE

There is, however, a "flip side" to this message. Keep in mind that people who have bipolar disorder have gifts and abilities that are often greater in quality and depth than others. Many talented people with mental disorders have changed our world for the better. Challenged by bipolar disorder, Winston Churchill demonstrated great leadership skills as the prime minister of England during World War II. He described his depression as a black dog that followed him everywhere. His political career was frequently stymied by his illness. He had even retired from political life when his country's citizens called him to lead them through their darkest hour. Indeed, he is known for his admonition to never give up. Here are his words, the entire text of a speech he gave to Harrow School:

Never give in.
Never give in.
Never, never, never, never—
In nothing great or small, large or petty,
Never give in
except to convictions of honor and good sense.

Abraham Lincoln was another great leader challenged by bipolar depression. At certain times, his friends never left him alone for fear he might kill himself. Describing his experience, Lincoln wrote:

> I am now the most miserable man living. If what I feel were equally distributed to the whole human family, there would be not one cheerful face on the earth. Whether I shall ever be better I cannot tell. I awfully forebode I shall not. To remain as I am is impossible. I must die or be better, it appears to me. *(Letter to John T. Stuart, January 23, 1841. Source: www.Lincolnportrait.com/essay2.ntm)*.

You might think that any president who had to cope with a civil war would feel this way. Soldiers and civilians of the North and South—all Americans—were dying in the thousands every day. However, as you can see from the date of the quotation above, he had depression long before he became president. His was not a passing "blue mood" caused by overworking, reading casualty reports and dealing with a myriad of stresses. Rather, depression affected Lincoln for virtually all of his adult life. Yet, in spite of it, this great leader piloted the nation through the stormy waters of its greatest test—determining whether the nation would remain united. He preserved the Union and in the process freed over three million slaves.

INNER STRENGTH TO PERSEVERE

Most of us will never become leaders of nations. However, we can learn from the lives of Churchill, Lincoln and others about the inner strength that enables people to persevere in spite of their challenges. Although you may not effect change on a planetary scale, you can have a powerful and lasting influence on those around you. You have special gifts and abilities to give you courage and creative ways of coping with bipolar disorder. This courage lets you move forward even when you feel permanently entangled and see no way out.

So in the midst of your illness, do not overlook the special gifts that make you the unique and creative person you are. These gifts provide the engine of hope as you move forward. And as you gain insight into bipolar disorder, you will have ample opportunity to discover the special giftedness that accompanies people who have this illness.

"Doc's" Story

Here I am, frightened, on the locked ward of a state mental hospital for the first time. I wonder how I will get through this. One thing reassures me. The doctor I am to see is a kind, soft-spoken man from India and Harvard trained in psychiatry. What could possibly have led him to the plains of South Dakota?

The sound of the door slamming behind me is cold and shocking, but few even seem to notice. The medical staff seems too busy to notice my arrival. The scene seems disconcerting to me: white walls, white tiled floor, standardized white furniture, TV blaring in a corner. I reach into my pocket. There they are. Within a few hours of my arrival, this action would become a ritual, a mantra, a rosary.

A few of the patients on the floor notice my entrance into their world. Some scare me. Quite a few have tremors or strange movements of their mouths and tongues that cause them to hide in the corners from embarrassment. Others have angry faces but speak little. Some move slowly. A few don't move at all. Still others talk rapidly and want to capture my attention. They stand unusually close as they begin one-way conversations. I don't know how to respond. But by the time I think of something to say, their attention has drifted. I perform my ritual of reaching into my pocket.

I am poorly prepared to be here in the acute ward of a state mental hospital. I feel alone and uncertain. However, I cling to the things that make me different from those around me. I perform my ritual of reaching nervously into my pocket. I walk anxiously down the hall and knock on the door of Dr. Mehta's office for our first appointment.

Our talk does little to allay my fears. Dr. Mehta asks me many questions. I learn the rules of the ward. He tells me to be cautious of a couple of patients whom I have already noticed. I sense Dr. Mehta's respect for them, but our conversation increases my anxiety. Ritualistically, I reach into my pocket.

My next appointment is with a young man named Paul, a college student spending his summer at the hospital. His job is to teach me the basics about bipolar disorder. By the end of the week, I feel comfortable during our talks. Paul likes to talk and that masks my shyness. Each day I have a session with Paul before seeing Dr. Mehta. I continue my ritual of reaching into my pocket but need this reassurance less frequently.

The first week passes. I feel more comfortable. I have improved and can even enjoy the company of several interesting people on the ward. Some seem like me, but I still reach into my pocket as a reminder of how we differ. This ritual has become comfortable.

At last, it's 4:00 pm on Friday. At the end of each day, reaching into my pocket is no longer a ritual. I now use the well-fingered keys to open the locked ward. I am different from those I see each day—I hold the keys! Gratefully, I unlock the door and leave behind the suffering of Paul and others whom I have met.

I find it strange that Paul calls me "Doc Jane." He and the other patients refuse to call me anything except "Doc" or "Doctor" no matter how frequently I remind them that I am a medical student, not a doctor. They easily accept the transformation that I am making from medical student to doctor. While I ritualistically cling to my keys, feeling fragile, they teach me that they—my patients—hold the true keys to my future as a physician. They teach me the art of my trade, for they know best the experience of illness.

Paul was my first patient as well as one of my first teachers. At the time, I only partially grasped the reality that Paul and I are not very different. We not only share a common humanity, but also the experience of having bipolar disorder. Even the ritual of fingering the keys in my pocket could not change that basic reality. Paul and others were teaching me first-hand knowledge, etching it deep into my memory. This knowledge of the experience of illness helped shaped my future both as a clinician and as a patient.

Defining Bipolar Disorder

BIPOLAR DISORDER, formerly known as manic-depression, is a neurobiologic disorder. *Neuro* means nerve or, in this case, brain. Biologic pertains to *living matter*. Thus the term neurobiologic confirms that bipolar disorder is a real physical condition involving the brain. It is not caused by a character flaw or laziness.

If you have bipolar disorder, you are not being moody on purpose, nor can you "snap out of it." Just as a person who has diabetes cannot at will "snap out of" having diabetes, you cannot snap out of the illness that you are experiencing. Well-meaning people may have advised you otherwise, but those same people would not ask you to snap out of having cancer, for example.

If you have bipolar disorder, that doesn't mean you can't take steps toward recovering from your illness. You may have trouble accepting you have a condition that prevents your brain from properly regulating your mood. You may be reeling from the powerful effect this disorder has had in your life. But learning more about bipolar disorder will help you manage this illness.

MEDICAL DEFINITION

So what is bipolar disorder anyway? I have already said it is a *neurobiologic* disorder, but that may mean little to you. Let's examine it from the medical point of view. As we go along, I will share some of my experiences as well as those from other physicians. That way, you can see how the medical characteristics of the disorder are affecting you.

SPECTRUM OF MOODS

Bipolar literally means *two poles,* implying that there are two basic "poles" or moods caused by the disorder. The opposite poles are severe depression and extreme mania or hypomania. While these two extremes may be present in your disorder, it's misleading to think of bipolar disorder in terms of extremes. It's more accurate to think of it as being a spectrum of disorders involving a wide range of moods.

At its core is the brain's inability to consistently regulate mood within a normal range. This inability of the brain to self-regulate mood results in varying degrees of depression, mania or hypomania. (Each of these moods is discussed separately in chapters that follow.) At times, a mixed mood can exist—a state that has elements of both depression and mania.

Earlier, I described bipolar disorder as a neurobiologic disorder. It is also sometimes called a brain disorder or a mental disorder. You may have already heard bipolar disorder described as involving a chemical imbalance in the brain. This understanding of the disorder stems from the fact that the medications used to treat bipolar disorder affect the brain's chemical make-up.

Bipolar disorder is medically classified, along with several other disorders, including major depression, as a mood disorder. However, as we shall see, the disorder affects far more than mood. Thus, it is misleading to regard bipolar disorder solely as a disturbance of mood.

DEFINING THE WORD "MOOD"

The word *mood* means much more than we may think. A simple Webster's dictionary definition of mood states that it is "a particular state of mind or feeling; humor, or temper." The word comes from older words meaning *mind, spirit, courage* and *to strive strongly, be energetic.* Therefore, when we think of mood, we may think in terms of how we feel—happy, sad, angry, elated, tired, content. But mood has an even broader meaning and encompasses much of what we need to go on living and succeeding.

Mood disorders affect us in many ways. They can rob us of mind, spirit, courage and strength. They can also enhance and intensify these qualities to enrich our lives.

Calling bipolar disorder a mood disorder, as the medical and clinical community has done, takes it beyond the realm of simply "affecting" how a person feels into a more complex realm.

Bipolar disorder is, at heart, a disorder that can cause emotional pain and can have a major impact on our lives because it involves the full range of the definition of mood.

Bipolar disorder is challenging but it also brings a wide range of gifts, including seeing the world from a new perspective—a perspective that most people probably miss. Life is experienced on a much more intense level.

TAKES ON A LIFE OF ITS OWN

If you have bipolar disorder, your mood sometimes takes on a life of its own, independent of what else is happening in your life. It becomes separate from your experiences. Dr. Francis Mondimore states this well in his book *Bipolar Disorder: A Guide for Patients and Families:*

> In mood disorders, the mood becomes disconnected from the individual's environment, and feelings of "happy" and "sad" take on rhythms and fluctuations of their own.... If the mood disorder patient and his or her situation are examined with enough care, however, the basic underlying problem will be found: a problem with regulation of mood. (*Bipolar Disorder: A Guide for Patients and Families,* p 8)

This "disconnecting" of mood from experience presents many trials in our daily lives. It can even affect the way we view ourselves as well as our self-confidence. Symptoms such as severe irritability can impair our interpersonal relationships. Sadness and hopelessness can become overwhelming and may even lead to suicide. We sometimes lose our sense of self. If our moods are unstable, we don't really know what we will be like when we wake up in the morning or later on in the day—or even in the next minute or hour.

Understanding that the core challenge in bipolar disorder is the brain's inability to self-regulate mood is crucial to dealing with the consequences of the disorder. When internal modulation (brain self-regulation) is not possible or is problematic, we have to look for other ways to modulate our moods. Unfortunately we sometimes turn to unhealthy coping techniques that may include blaming others, isolating ourselves or using drugs and/or alcohol to feel better.

Ways to Regulate Mood

Use of medications and treatments often provides effective ways to manage extremes of moods. We can also learn external techniques to manage these extremes or to work around our brains' inefficient mood-regulation system. For example, when we feel anxious, we might get relief by talking with someone about our anxieties. Another person's assurance can help calm us when our brains have difficulty modulating anxious thoughts and feelings.

We may also feel relief by writing down a list of triggers that are increasing our anxieties. Reviewing the list, we can add reasons why our fears are unrealistic. Or if our fears are realistic, we can take action instead of feeling overwhelmed by them.

When we become irritable, we may like to be held by a loved one or to go for a walk or take some deep breaths. Any of these help modulate moods, bypassing the brain's extremes.

Summary

We have learned that bipolar disorder is classified as a mood disorder and that the word *mood* implies more than a range of feelings. We have also learned that the core of bipolar disorder is the brain's inability to consistently regulate mood within normal bounds.

Understanding What Normal Means

C LINICIANS DEFINE three main moods that may be present in bipolar disorders—depression, mania and hypomania. We also need to consider a fourth mood, "normal." All four of these moods are diagramed in Figure 1 *(p 30)* so you can visualize them.

First of all, notice that the letters spelling "normal mood" in the diagram vary slightly in that they curve up and down. This illustrates that "normal" is not stagnant, but that it has its lows and highs. Perhaps we know someone whose mood is steady all the time, but this is unusual. Look at a couple of examples to see what I mean.

DOWN BUT NOT DEPRESSED

Let's say your mood is normal and one day you have an argument with your boss. Consequently, you dread going to work the next morning. You may arrive and tell a co-worker you are feeling "down" or even "depressed." Later that day, you talk with your boss and find out things weren't as bad as you had feared. You straighten out the problem and then feel better.

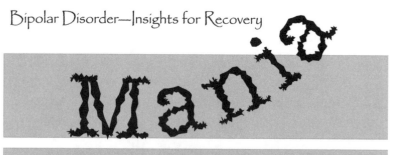

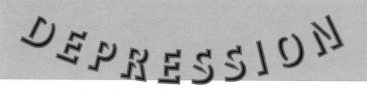

Figure 1—The Four Moods

Notice that you described your mood as being "depressed." We might understand what you mean, but this is not true clinical depression. In fact, describing "down" feelings as depression does a disservice to those of us who experience clinical depression. This leaves the impression that true clinical depression is just a mild, passing mood. True depression is far more intense; technically, it must last at least two weeks before a diagnosis can be made.

Let's look at another example. You usually experience a normal mood but maybe you stayed up too late last night and awoke tired and a little blue. Perhaps you decide to cheer yourself up by going out to lunch with friends. Part way through lunch, you realize you are no longer feeling blue.

What you experienced was a "blue mood" that came and went. This falls within the range of "normal" mood and is not considered clinical depression for two reasons. First, it was not a severe mood (as I will describe later) and it did not last for at least two weeks. Second, your ability to devise and enjoy finding a solution for your blue mood shows a resilience that's not associated with clinical depression. You were able to "snap out of it" without much difficulty.

For those of us with true depression, things do not work quite this easily. Our brains cannot consistently regulate mood within a normal range. For this reason, I always encourage people with normal mood to say they are in a "blue mood" rather than use the word "depressed." There is no comparison.

Likewise, mania and hypomania are not the same as the elation associated with normal mood. Attending a football game may cause a feeling of elation among people in an enthusiastic crowd when their team wins. Getting a new job to replace the one you dreaded each morning might cause you to glow with joy if your mood is in the normal range. These emotions are neither as extreme as the moods of mania and hypomania, nor do they last long enough to qualify as mania or hypomania. They illustrate the resiliency of normal mood.

A PSYCHIATRIST'S LESSON

Although I had been taught about clinical depression in medical school, I had to learn the distinction between a normal mood and depression from my psychiatrist.

When choosing a psychiatrist, I had an advantage over others because of my professional associations. I had already known my doctor and his top-notch reputation before I went to him for treatment. Indeed, we had already established a level of mutual respect and trust.

When I began seeing my doctor for treatment for bipolar disorder, he talked at length about normal mood. One day, he said something that totally astounded me. He told me that most people feel happy most of the time!

It was as though he'd said we were standing on the planet Mars or something equally unbelievable. I actually wondered if he needed treatment for delusional thinking! The idea of being happy or content most of the time went so far beyond my life experience that I thought he must be living in a fairy tale.

HAPPY MOST OF THE TIME? IMPOSSIBLE!

Most people are happy most of the time? No way! This simply had not been my experience from early childhood on. I could not fathom such a thing, and I wouldn't believe my psychiatrist without checking it out myself. So I conducted an informal poll of everyone I saw for the next few days. I asked friends, patients, employees and people from my church—everyone I ran into—if they felt happy most of the time. The majority of them thought for a few seconds, maybe scratched their chins, but in the end they all said "yes."

Now, I don't pretend I conducted a scientific poll, but it was enough to convince me that my reality had been skewed by the mood disorder I was experiencing. This general state of happiness was such a novel concept that it took me a long time and a lot of observation to understand what a normal mood is. Since then, I have seen scientific studies showing that most people are indeed happy or content most of the time.

When I studied and practiced medicine as a family physician, I first learned about "normal" human anatomy, physiology and behavior. It was later in my training that I learned about diseases and disorders. By understanding what was normal or usual, I was able to understand the contrast of biologic diseases and disorders. Textbooks taught me a lot, but I also learned early on that I could best understand diseases and disorders by learning from patients who were experiencing what I was reading about. Thus my patients taught me how to be a doctor by sharing their experiences with me.

EXPERIENCE IS OUR TEACHER

Here's the lesson: If you want to learn more about bipolar disorder, ask those who experience it. Just as it was difficult for me to understand a normal mood, so it will be difficult for anyone who has never experienced depression, mania or hypomania to understand the extremes of moods described in this book. These moods will seem totally mysterious, just as a normal mood had been a mystery to me.

And if you have bipolar disorder, it will help if you can get a sense of what a normal mood is like. In doing so, you can also assist your doctor or therapist to better understand where you are with the experience of bipolar illness.

Gaining insight in this way takes you toward your recovery process. The next step is learning about depression, mania and hypomania.

The Depression Puzzle Piece

IN THE LAST chapter, we talked about "blue mood" and how it is different from depression, both in intensity and in duration. Figure 2 *(p 36)* illustrates that depression is a distinct mood. With depression, common emotions include feelings of sadness, worthlessness and hopelessness. You may notice these features when you are depressed, but be aware that people experience depression in different ways.

However, if we think of a puzzle with many pieces, we don't have to have every piece in place to tell what the picture is. Depression is like this. You might have some of the pieces to the puzzle while others will have entirely different pieces.

There can be radical differences in how individuals experience depression. These differences occur between men and women, children, adults and older adults as well as among people of differing cultures, race and color. But if puzzle pieces of depression are present for at least two weeks, the big picture will reveal a diagnosis of clinical depression.

This chapter takes some of the emotional, cognitive (thinking) and vegetative features of the depression puzzle and looks at them closely so we can better recognize depression.

Figure 2—Depression

EMOTIONAL FEATURES

Emotional features of depression include sadness, tearfulness, irritability and anhedonia.

Sadness

If you have bipolar depression, you may experience sadness differently from someone without this disorder. Very likely, your sadness is far more intense than sadness in others. Not only is it unusually intense, but it also lasts longer. Everyday sadness of normal mood comes and goes and is punctuated with periods of relative happiness.

Your sadness may cause you to cry at length or isolate yourself. It may affect your social skills to the point that you withdraw from others whose company you normally enjoy. Although you may appear to lead a normal life, you feel overwhelmingly sad most of the time for as long as the depression lasts.

Tearfulness

Tearfulness is when you start crying for no special reason and do not have control over your tears. Little things that ordinarily would not make you cry trigger a crying spell. This often happens when I go to the movies while I am experiencing depression. Oddly enough, I am able to watch a tearjerker with dry eyes but burst into tears when the credits appear on the screen. Somehow the thought of all those people being involved in the making of a movie triggers a crying spell that I can't control.

At times, a phrase or a question may trigger my sobs. I cry easily when I am angry or when I hear something that is emotionally charged. While crying itself is not abnormal, crying with little or no provocation is a common piece of the depression puzzle. Prolonged crying spells nearly always indicate depression.

Irritability and anxiety

As with sadness, it is the intensity and duration of your irritability that distinguishes it from the occasional irritability of others. The irritability of depression is also coupled with anxiety. Your anxiety may not have a specific cause; often it is present no matter what your outward circumstances. Of those who experience depression, men, adolescents and children are more likely to experience irritability more than other common symptoms of depression.

Anhedonia (loss of enjoyment)

Anhedonia means an inability to take pleasure in normally pleasurable activities. It literally means *without pleasure.* Though it can refer to sexual pleasure, anhedonia also refers to any pleasurable activity. When you are depressed, you may not be able to enjoy the things you normally do, such as going to a movie with friends or working out at the gym. You may even find yourself withdrawing from others by turning down invitations. Or you may not want to take on that new project at work or school, even though it is something you usually enjoy. You may keep up your usual activities but without enjoyment. To some, anhedonia feels like an intense boredom with activities that would normally elicit pleasure.

In the example noted in the last chapter, going out to lunch lifted that person out of a blue mood due to an ability to enjoy time with friends. Unfortunately, when you are experiencing depression, others may encourage you to become more active with the hope that this will lift your mood out of depression. Yet you may not be able to enjoy the activities because you lack the ability to experience pleasure.

Does this mean you should shy away from activities? Certainly not! But realize that you need to choose them carefully with an understanding of the amount of stimulation you can tolerate. This tolerance varies from person to person and at different times of the day during an episode of depression.

Little Activities Can Mean a Lot

When disability turned my life upside down, what I learned from my Aunt Donna Cooley kept me going through the darkest days. Her homespun hope for the future helped me put one foot in front of the other on my own journey.

I remember the day I first saw Aunt Donna's button collection. Gallon jars of buttons collected and sorted by color for over 50 years lured my eyes and made my hands itch to enjoy the feel of cool buttons falling through my fingers.

Two of my young cousins came by that day. Because I was ill and they were immersed in their eleven-year-old world, conversation during dinner was scant. Indeed, I had lost the ability to enjoy the company of youth that formerly had been one of my greatest joys.

After supper, Aunt Donna plopped her six-ounce jar of buttons before the three of us and told us to get busy sorting. Soon we were engrossed in choosing buttons, each sharing a favorite with the others. We shared stories about our lives as well. We all connected and it felt good.

Learning to enjoy simple pleasures like this has helped me live with the chronic illness that challenges me. Aunt Donna's buttons of friendship give me support as well as happy memories in spite of the sadness I sometimes feel.

START FROM WHERE YOU ARE RIGHT NOW

If you are experiencing depression, your challenge for the day may be simply to get up and brush your teeth or take a shower. That challenge may not seem like much to someone else, but never mind. If taking a shower is difficult for you and you do it anyway, praise yourself. You have accomplished more than you thought you could. And remember, no law says you have to enjoy what you do. When you feel better, your challenges will be different. You can only start from where you are right now.

ADD STRUCTURE TO YOUR DAY

Ask yourself what activities normally energize you, then complete one such activity each day. You may find this helpful because it gives structure to your day. It could simply be calling a friend, going for a walk or writing in your journal.

Once when I was experiencing a severe depression for a long period of time, I made a commitment to get out of the house each day. At times, all I did was get on the bus and ride three miles to downtown, then back home. At least this got me around other people without requiring me to carry on extensive social interactions. The scenery differed from my customary surroundings, and observing people from every walk of life provided education and even entertainment.

I also walked my dog in the park and sang hymns over and over, looking at the neighbors' gardens on the way. This got me through many difficult times, even though I didn't enjoy it. Still, I felt a bit more human than if I had stayed home and slept all day as I desperately wanted to.

COGNITIVE FEATURES

Cognitive refers to a person's thinking. Some of the most common cognitive features of depression are poor concentration, a sense of worthlessness and feelings of hopelessness. These are described below.

Concentration

Concentrating means paying attention to what you are doing so you can complete simple or complex tasks without forgetting what you are doing. Depression tends to make you turn inward, and because of this, you may have difficulty focusing on things happening around you.

Unfortunately, your inability to concentrate can wreak havoc on your life, work and relationships. For instance, meeting new people requires you to remember their names and focus on conversation. Conversing with others obliges you to concentrate well enough to express your thoughts clearly.

When you are having difficulties focusing, a simple trip to the grocery store suddenly becomes more difficult. You may forget what you came for or you may pass the fruit section without picking up the bananas you had planned to buy. You might even go by the store, but pass it altogether. You may even have to backtrack blocks or even miles because you forgot where you were going.

Concentration is needed for most jobs. If you can't concentrate, your productivity decreases. This is why depression is one of the top ten causes of disability and lack of productivity in the workplace. According to the World Health Organization (WHO), depression is expected to be the leading cause of disability worldwide by the year 2020. Currently, it is second only to cardiovascular disease in the industrialized world.

You can address the challenge with concentration difficulties by making lists of things to do. The major drawback to lists is that you can easily lose them, so make sure you tape them down in some way. (I sometimes use giant sticky notes on which I can put a whole week's activities.) Using organizers, calendars or Personal Data Assistants (PDA's) are also an option.

Consider decreasing the amount of stimulation in your environment. Do you really need to have the TV or radio on all the time? Can you ask for a workspace that is away from the crowd? (In fact, such accommodations are required in most work settings by the Americans with Disabilities Act or the Federal Rehabilitation Act of 1973 and subsequent revisions.)

A simple way to increase your focus is to spend a few minutes many times each day just thinking about your breath going in and out. Take very slow, deep breaths from the bottom of your abdomen and focus on the air going in and out. Don't fall into the trap of saying you have to take ten deep breaths! When I try this I lose count around three, thus throwing all concentration to the wind. When you're breathing, think about your breath moving in and out.

Sense of worthlessness

A sense of feeling worthless can take many forms, including a belief that you cannot do things right, that you have no friends or that you are a failure in life. Notice that I am using the word *belief* to describe this cognitive feature. That is because a sense of worthlessness may have nothing to do with the reality of your accomplishments or the number of friends you have. You may have an abundance of people close to you, but when you are experiencing depression, you may believe beyond a doubt that you are totally alone in the world.

When I am in the deep hole of depression, I can give you a hundred reasons why it is unreasonable to believe that anyone cares about me. My depression speaks loudly and convincingly. The cognitive feature of a sense of worthlessness has everything to do with delusional thinking that can accompany depression.

You can learn not to listen to this kind of thinking by proposing alternative thoughts to yourself. One of the best responses is to make a list of your friends, or better yet, call one of them. I find calling friends to be very difficult and it may be difficult for you as well. However, it is hard to continue the delusion of having no friends when you are talking with one!

Still can't believe you have any friends? Then list the qualities you have that make you likeable. Still need more convincing? Check out Cognitive Behavioral Therapy. This therapy helps you question your distorted beliefs about yourself, events and others. It helps you develop alternative, healthier explanations than those coming from depression. If you cannot find anyone who does this type of therapy or if you can't afford it, work through some self-help books. (See the back of this book.)

Hopelessness

Why include hopelessness as a thinking feature of depression? Isn't it more like an emotion rather than a thinking problem?

Overwhelming hopelessness feels extremely painful. But it is the thoughts that accompany our hopelessness that become dangerous to others and to ourselves. Thinking that suicide or even homicide is a reasonable way to deal with the intense pain you feel is a cognitive feature of extreme depression. Realize that these thoughts are abnormal, no matter how much they make sense at the time. They result from the depression over-riding normal hopes and desires that preserve your life.

Like breathing, hope is necessary to life. In depression, hopelessness can become extreme. When you are in this place, you may be in so much emotional pain that you do not want to experience its intensity for one more hour, one more minute or even one more second. Coupled with opportunity and choice, this intensity of pain can lead to suicide.

During times when hopelessness takes over, you need to be in a safe place with close friends and family who are capable of monitoring your behavior. You may need hospitalization to ensure you have a safe place until the hopelessness passes.

So when you are in this state of utter hopelessness, ask for help from someone who knows how to help, even though this may be difficult for you. This person might be your psychiatrist, your therapist or a trusted friend who cares about you.

Alternatively, you can call a suicide hotline (1.800.suicide) or dial 911. Keep in your purse or wallet a note that says, "I am feeling suicidal. I need help." Sometime when you are feeling in control, show the note to a few trusted people and give them instructions. Use it if you feel suicidal but are unable to ask for help.

Know about other resources in your community. The Yellow Ribbon Suicide Prevention Program is part of the Light for

Life Foundation International. High school students who were concerned after a classmate completed suicide founded this organization. Volunteers for this group hand out wallet cards that explain how to get help.

VEGETATIVE FEATURES

You may have heard the term "veg out." Maybe you asked a friend what he did over the weekend and he replied that he didn't do much, just "vegged out."

With the vegetative features of depression, "vegging out" takes on a whole new level of meaning! These features include extreme lack of energy and disturbance of sleep.

Lack of energy

When you are experiencing depression, your energy decreases. It often appears as an overwhelming tiredness and may become extreme to the point of not being able to get out of bed. When you experience depression, simple things such as getting dressed or brushing your teeth seem impossible because they take more energy than you have. Small projects seem infinite in the time and energy that they will take to even start, much less finish.

You may slow down to the point that you can hardly move. A careful observer will notice that you lack energy and talk and move more slowly than normal. This is called *psychomotor retardation* because it is a brain function *(psycho)* that affects your motion *(motor)* to slow down *(retard)* your body.

When you are slowed down like this, mobilization—getting back to normal activities—is important for recovery. You can increase mobilization by setting realistic goals. Notice I said "setting realistic goals," not "having guilt-inducing expectations imposed on you." For instance, a simple activity like taking a five-minute walk or a twenty-minute ride in the car may be a realistic goal for an individual who has this feature of depression. An all-day outing to the ballpark is most likely unreasonable, even though an important person in your life may push you to try this or other similar activities.

Disturbance in sleep

Depression often causes sleep problems called *hyposomnia* and *hypersomnia*. Hyposomnia can take quite a few forms. In some cases, it may be an inability to fall asleep at night, called difficulty falling asleep or DFA. Although DFA is more frequently associated with anxiety than with depression, it can occur with either. Middle of the night awakening (MNA) and early morning awakening (EMA) are more frequently found with depression. (Notice that these symptoms are so common, the medical community has assigned them acronyms!)

Hyposomnia associated with depression is usually accompanied by fatigue. As we will see later, this is not true in cases of hyposomnia associated with hypomania or mania. With mania, you're not sleeping but have all the energy in the world. With depression, you're tired.

Hypersomnia is another sleep disturbance and is the opposite of hyposomnia. In depression characterized by hypersomnia, you may sleep for twelve or fourteen hours a day, but in spite of all that sleep you still feel exhausted. That's because the sleep doesn't restore your energy and refresh your mind. When

I experience depression, I can sleep all night and most of the day. When this happens, my cat and I become close friends and snooze together on the couch until the sun goes down. We awaken to eat a bit and then hurry to bed before we fall asleep again!

While we are on the topic of eating, note that in depression your appetite may be greatly affected. You might eat too much or too little. Thus weight gain or weight loss can be experienced with depression.

SUMMARY

We have discussed several features of depression including emotional, cognitive and vegetative features. These are not a complete list of the symptoms of depression, but when we put these symptoms together like pieces in a puzzle, we can recognize the overall picture of depression. Next, let's look at mania and hypomania to get insight into these moods.

The Black Bird That Dogs Me

Churchill described living with depression as having a black dog that followed him wherever he went. I think of my illness as the black bird that dogs me.

When I walk in the park, I feel especially blessed when I see my favorite bird, the Cormorant, on the lake. On a good day, I am like this black bird, floating deep in the water, dipping my whole being into the waters of life. But the Cormorant is unlike the geese and ducks that inhabit the same lake; it does not float upon the water but rather in it. That is how I yearn to be, so much a part of life that I am nearly sinking in its essence.

The Cormorant appeals because of its differences from other waterfowl—it "lacks." This black bird lacks the water repelling oils that keep the other birds afloat above the water, causing it to sink nearly to its shoulders. Its long neck shows above water as if proud of its failure to be overcome by the water's drowning edge! This lack is its gift.

I also have a lack that leaves me sinking deeply into life—a lack of brain chemistry that causes my depressions. On a good day, this lack leaves me floating deeply and experiencing life from a different vantage. I can look far above the water but at the same time I am engulfed by life.

On a good day.

The Cormorant dives, head first, sinking low in search of fish. Its unoiled wings and sleek build allow it to disappear for minutes. When will it return and what the prize, if any?

I too will dive and sink, the world surrounding me and I lacking buoyancy. How deep the depression? Like the Cormorant, no one knows where I shall again appear.

After spreading its oil-less wings to dry, the Cormorant flies, goose-like but silent. Like the Cormorant, I too fly silently, unaware of the eyes that watch me.

The Cormorant is the black bird that dogs me. I cannot escape the dogging, for my illness is always with me. I fly noiselessly and I sink to the depths, returning with what, I don't know. I float surrounded, unprotected from life, with shoulders, neck and head lending a brave prospective.

I watch my favorite bird that dogs me, hating the lack in brain chemistry that makes me so different—so lacking compared to others, yet at times cherishing the heights and depths I obtain that force me to spread my wings toward worlds of enrichment.

Just as I watch and find pleasure in the Cormorant's individuality, so there is One who watches me and finds pleasure in my special gifts. Only that One knows with what prize I return from the depths—and what flight transforms my character beyond the skies.

The Mania/Hypomania Puzzle Piece

Having examined some of the puzzle pieces of depression in the previous chapter, we add mania and hypomania to the picture of bipolar disorder in this chapter. As before, we will not look at every possible puzzle piece but instead cover enough important ones to put all of these pieces together and form a picture that's recognized as bipolar disorder. We will discuss mania and hypomania together, viewing them as different expressions of the same feature.

Between "Normal" and "Mania"

Looking at the diagram of mania and hypomania in Figure 3 *(p 52)*, notice that hypomania occupies a narrower box than mania. It is easily hidden between normal mood and mania so it sometimes gets overlooked. If you are challenged by hypomania, you know it is possible to hide symptoms of hypomania from people around you. This is because the features of hypomania are not quite as obvious as the symptoms of mania. However, this does not mean the symptoms are not as emotionally painful. It just means they can be easily hidden.

Figure 3—Hypomania/Mania

You may have been treated previously for depression, but your symptoms of hypomania were missed altogether. Either you weren't asked the right questions or were diagnosed before doctors became widely aware of this feature of bipolar disorder. Or you may have had a pattern of bipolar disorder that is largely characterized by depression. Thus, bipolar disorder that has hypomania as one feature can easily masquerade as unipolar depression, that is, a depressive disorder that lacks the additional "pole" of mania or hypomania. Unipolar depression is what most people mean when using the word *depression*.

Looking at Figure 3 again, notice that mania didn't fit into its box in spite of my best efforts to make it fit. Indeed, I realized that mania does not fit easily into any box. That's because it's an expansive mood waiting to be noticed. Even the untrained can observe its features.

When you experience mania, you are riding high and living far outside the boundaries of a normal mood. Rather than hiding from the world, you are likely to flaunt your mania, so much so that you can get noticed in ways you later regret. In this case, illness often gets discovered more quickly and because of that, treatment for bipolar disorder begins earlier. However, because mania involves an expansive, pleasurable mood, you may resist seeking treatment. Also it is often difficult for you to recognize mania even when you are experiencing it. Learning to identify your symptoms is an important step in understanding your illness.

From here on, I will refer to mania and hypomania together, classifying them both as "mania," acknowledging their similarities despite their subtle differences. For now, just remember that there used to be only one identified type of bipolar disorder, but with growing understanding of the disorder there are newer classifications that include Bipolar I Disorder and Bipolar II Disorder.

Bipolar I is characterized by episodes of mania as well as episodes of depression. Bipolar II is a depressive illness with episodes of depression and episodes of hypomania. Cyclothymic Disorder, a third type of bipolar disorder, is a chronic disorder with numerous fluctuations between features of depression and hypomania but lacking the clear episodes of either depression or hypomania.

However, all contain features of depression and features of either hypomania or mania.

EMOTIONAL FEATURES

Common emotional features of mania include unstable mood and irritability.

Unstable mood

The hallmark of mania is experiencing an unstable mood, an exercise of "catch as catch can" because your mood shifts rapidly between extremes. For instance, you may have a sudden burst of energy with loud laughter, joke telling and performances for everyone. But within a short time, your mood or attention shifts to something different. You are unable to sit still so you stop performing and do something else that catches your attention.

Irritability

The irritability of depression as described in the last chapter has an anxious quality. If you experience mania, your irritability is characterized by low frustration tolerance. You can become easily frustrated and lose control. You might feel so irritable that you want to crawl out of your skin.

When I feel irritable, it builds and builds, often erupting in the "big TT" (temper tantrum). Although I can usually control this behavior in public, it wreaks havoc on my home life. (We often feel safest unleashing our illness around those closest to us.)

Anger versus irritability

What is the difference between anger and irritability? Anger has a specific target while irritability has no particular focus. The target of anger could be another person's actions, a circumstance or a perceived failure.

The irritability of mania is generalized and volatile. When you have it—the kind of irritability in which you want to crawl out of your skin—you have low tolerance for frustration. All it takes is one small trigger (which could be anything) to cause a major explosion. The trigger doesn't even have to be pulled; just being near it is enough to set off the fireworks!

When you feel irritable, you may not realize your voice sounds sharp and your speech inappropriately loud. You're surprised by your sudden outburst of uncontrollable temper. Obviously, such behavior can strain relationships, especially if your irritability is interpreted as anger.

A person or situation around you can easily become a target for your irritability. Try to get through one of those awful telephone trees in which you have to choose from a number of choices when you are feeling this way! It shows incredible restraint if you can get to the third choice without hanging up or yelling, "I want to speak to a live person!"

It's critical to see the irritability of mania for what it is—an emotional feature that stems from your brain's inability to consistently regulate mood within a normal range. This insight allows you and those around you to deal with irritability in a positive way. Often others recognize your irritability before you do. Ask them in advance to tell you when they notice irritability before it builds out of control. You may have to teach them how to do this, but it is well worth the effort because you can then take steps to manage your irritability before it escalates.

Remember, it is not fair to complain and deny your irritability when someone points it out. Instead, do your best to stop reacting and take steps to calm down. It is also unfair for family or friends to use the slightest sign of irritability as an explanation for every relationship challenge to the family or friendship.

What can you do to calm down? When you feel irritable, you can take a long walk, do deep breathing exercises or back away from a frustrating activity. Simply acknowledging irritability may help you deal with it more constructively than moving on to the "big TT" (temper tantrum).

Practice skills to modulate irritability so you are prepared to manage your irritable moods. If you think you can't use calming techniques because you explode into tantrums without warning, remember that acknowledging this tendency is the first step toward management. Use techniques such as deep breathing throughout the day to moderate your irritability and thus decrease its power over you. Choose activities low in frustration and take time alone instead of staying in the fray of a challenge. For instance, reading a book or going for a walk may be safer than trying to solve the computer glitch that's annoying you.

Cognitive Features

Common cognitive features of mania are gradiosity, poor judgement, disorganization and rapid speech/racing thoughts.

Grandiosity

When you experience grandiosity, your opinion about yourself is inflated and you are convinced you can do impossible things. While feeling grandiose, you might believe you can climb Mount Everest, even though you have never set foot on a mountain. You may think you can reach the summit in three days without preparation or training—and without a guide!

Though this example sounds preposterous, it is certainly not beyond the extremes of grandiosity that can accompany mania. On a more subtle level, grandiosity makes goals seem more attainable than they actually are. For example, you may believe you can do a six-month project in three days or accomplish a month's worth of gardening in a day.

In contrast, having difficulty with planning works in reverse when you are experiencing depression. For example, you may not attempt even the simplest project since you believe that a three-day project will take six months to finish. Clearly, an individual with bipolar disorder faces challenges in setting and reaching realistic goals.

Poor judgment

Mania can impair your judgment to the extent that you are unable to realistically weigh the consequences of your actions. For instance, your high energy level and grandiosity may lead to spending sprees, which are commonly seen with mania. You may run up outrageous credit card debt resulting in financial disaster. You may write bad checks to cover your debts. Normally, your ability to foresee the consequences would allow you to curb this behavior. In fact, your judgment can be impaired to the extent that you do not even consider the consequences of your actions.

Such lack of judgment coupled with difficulty in controlling impulses leads to big trouble. To counteract this, you can plan in advance. For example, when you show symptoms of mania, you can cancel your credit cards or turn them (with your checkbook) over to a trusted person. Again, having insight into your symptoms is an important step toward preventing problems. It allows you to manage your symptoms early so that others don't feel that they need to step in to control things.

When experiencing mania, you can also put yourself in danger by driving recklessly or showing poor judgment in forming relationships with strangers. You may be driven by the grandiosity already described but at the same time, lack the restraint normal judgment would provide. At these times, share your plans with a trusted person who can help you see the consequences of your actions.

When your judgment is impaired by mania, you may have to rely more heavily on the judgment of others until you feel better. For instance, instead of going shopping when you experience mania, go to a friend's house, a clubhouse, a gym or a drop-in center. You might also call your doctor or even check into a day care program or hospital.

When you experience mania, it is difficult to identify it, so having a list of symptoms handy can help you recognize mania sooner and take action. Writing plans for dealing with symptoms is key to managing your illness. Prepare management action plans in advance, write them down, review them daily and immediately act when symptoms appear.

The Wellness Recovery Action Plan (WRAP) developed by Mary Ellen Copeland is a valuable resource to help you do this. WRAP is taught in seminars in many local communities and you can also purchase workbooks to help you develop a WRAP plan. (See Recovery Resources, pp 141-143.)

Disorganization

When you experience this feature of mania, you could end up with a whirlwind of clutter strewn from one end of your workspace to the other. It extends from your home to your car, garage and everywhere you go. You may have difficulty doing simple planning because of your decreased ability to organize. While a feature of mania is increased energy that sometimes leads to high levels of productivity, your focus can be so intense that it creates a stream of cast-off, unfinished activities meandering through your workspace. It's as though organization is held captive by activity.

During these times, be sure to remind yourself to finish each activity before starting another. Have someone organize your workspace so you can gain clarity to function efficiently. Or limit your workspace to a manageable area rather than spreading out throughout the entire house.

Rapid speech/racing thoughts

When you have these features, you may not perceive them as "rapid" or "racing." Instead, you believe the rest of the world has slowed down. What's more, your thoughts may become very intrusive and you can't stay on topic. Because concentration and ability to focus are affected, you may simultaneously begin a number of projects without finishing ones you've already started. For example, when I am reading several books at the same time, I know I am experiencing mania. When I can't read at all, I know that my mania has progressed to an even higher level.

Remember, racing thoughts may be hard to identify. Instead, you may just believe your mind is thinking of more things than you could ever describe. Alternately, this rush of thoughts or speech may be intrusive, keeping your mind distracted from what you need to concentrate on.

PHYSIOLOGIC FEATURES

Physiologic features include disturbance in sleep, high energy level and psychomotor agitation.

Disturbance in sleep

Typical sleep patterns in depression include hyposomnia or hypersomnia. The main sleep feature of mania is little need for sleep or hyposomnia. The hyposomnia in depression is accompanied by fatigue while hyposomnia or difficulty sleeping found in mania is characterized by a high energy level. Loss of sleep may not be extreme, especially in hypomania, but the accompanying feature is a high energy level.

High energy level

The high energy levels that accompany mania can lead to prolific accomplishments. However, mania can also lead to self-destructive behavior. You can be extremely productive if you experience hyposomnia. You have tremendous energy with an ability to think and work rapidly. If you can channel these attributes, you can accomplish things that a person with normal moods cannot begin to match. This is one reason why some individuals with bipolar disorder can be highly successful.

The works of some of the greatest artists, musicians and politicians have taken place during an episode of mania or hypomania. Robert Schumann, for instance, sketched out his first symphony in three days in the high-octane surge we now call mania.

Your challenge when experiencing mania is to direct your high energy level toward constructive activities. Those who do this often achieve success in their endeavors. However, if you let your mania go full bore with no constructive direction, it's like winding up a tightly coiled spring. When the spring loses the energy of the mania, you can find yourself slipping back into depression. That's why it's important to balance high energy with calming exercises.

It can be helpful, then, to keep a lid on your high energy level. Curtail your activities by taking breaks throughout the day and avoiding over-stimulation. This is the time when decreasing stimulation such as loud music is helpful. Short breaks to relax or take a walk will help tame the energy of mania without decreasing your productivity. Be productive, but don't fuel the mania.

Since mania with high productivity may be followed by periods of depression with low productivity, people with bipolar disorder benefit by having flexible jobs that allow for highly productive periods coupled with down periods. Such flexibility not only maximizes productivity, it also helps avoid getting overly stressed.

"Slow is real." Repeating this statement whenever your energy level causes you to race can help you get a perspective on things. Remember, the rest of the world is not operating at your furious pace. Rein in your high spirits for at least a few minutes each hour so that you don't fuel the symptoms of mania. In doing so you will be better able to make your creativity and energy work *for you* instead of *against you.*

Psychomotor agitation

This is the opposite of the psychomotor retardation of depression. With the psychomotor agitation of mania, you may not be able to sit still. You may twiddle your thumbs, jiggle your knee or fidget. You may be constantly in motion. Walking fast or running may feel good to you.

Here, too, finding a balance is important. Some people fuel mania with extreme exercise. Exercise can help, but choose an exercise such as walking that calms rather than feeds mania.

As with irritability, going for walks and deep breathing can be helpful management tools for these symptoms. However, if you are on the move and cannot stop, call your doctor or therapist or ask someone else to call for help.

PSYCHOSIS

Another symptom could be a psychosis such as hearing or seeing things that are not present. If you are experiencing milder forms of these features, you may not even be aware of flashes of lights at the side of your visual field. You may occasionally think you are hearing your name called out even though no one is there.

In more extreme forms, psychosis can include seeing people or things that are not there or hearing voices that say more than just your name. Consequently, you may become paranoid or afraid of others. You may feel compelled to do things that you normally would not do. If you have these symptoms, call your doctor immediately or dial 911 if you might be a danger to yourself or others. If the situation has progressed this far, others will likely have to intervene because you may have difficulty discerning what is real versus what are symptoms.

EUPHORIC & DYSPHORIC

Mania is most often thought of as euphoric or pleasurable. However, it can also be experienced as a dysphoric or unpleasant. Feeling so irritable that you could crawl out of your skin is dysphoric. Although nobody knows why, hypomania can often be dysphoric, especially in women.

If you experience euphoria, you may see little or no need for treatment and may even avoid it—especially the part about taking medications—like the plague. This avoidance indicates you need to work toward developing insight into your experience of bipolar disorder. While euphoria may feel good, mania disrupts many aspects of your life and can be disastrous for your relationships. The depression that naturally follows euphoria in the course of the illness is anything but pleasurable. In its extremes, it can be life threatening.

Don't make the mistake of thinking that only the depression

can be treated without treating the mania. Seek treatment and stay in treatment to maintain the best stability in your life. Creativity and high productivity do not have to be sacrificed in order to obtain successful treatment. In fact, appropriate treatment should enhance these qualities.

SUMMARY

Features of mania can include an expansive, unstable mood with hyposomnia characterized by a high energy level. Irritability with a low frustration threshold is often present, as well as grandiosity, poor judgment and disorganization. Psychomotor agitation and psychotic features may also be a part of mania. Increased productivity in goal-directed activities is often a feature.

All of these are parts of the puzzle for mania but, as with depression, each piece is not always present. Yet the overall picture can be recognized even though some pieces may be missing.

So far we have examined normal mood in order to give us a baseline against which to compare depression and mania. We then reviewed several puzzle pieces for both depression and mania. These lead to a better understanding of bipolar disorder and how it is diagnosed.

In the next chapter, we will put together the pieces of the depression and mania puzzles.

How Diagnoses Are Made

WE HAVE examined some of the puzzle pieces of both depression and mania. Now it's time to put the pieces together and form a broader picture that describes bipolar disorder.

As we have learned throughout our journey, not all of the same pieces for the puzzle apply to everyone. But to have a diagnosis of bipolar disorder, enough pieces must be present so that the overall picture can be recognized.

Do you wonder about the subjectivity of this process? Does it sound as though a diagnosis is being pulled out of thin air? Do you ever wonder whether someone has made a mistake about diagnosis, even if you recognize some of the features of depression or mania in yourself? If you have been given other diagnoses in the past or if bipolar disorder has been recently diagnosed, you may question whether the diagnosis is correct. These important questions deserve attention.

This chapter helps you understand how a diagnosis is made and how doctors and mental health clinicians put the puzzle together. If you question a diagnosis at any point, ask how the conclusion was reached. If you are still uncertain, get a second opinion. Because effective treatment is closely linked with a correct diagnosis, pursue the answers to your questions to ensure that you and your clinician are on the right track.

BIPOLAR DISORDER SYNDROME

Medically, bipolar disorder is described as a syndrome. The word syndrome comes from *syn* (with) and *dramein* (to run). A syndrome is defined as a number of symptoms occurring together that characterize a specific disease or condition. Before modern-day medicine, many disorders were diagnosed by putting symptoms and observations together like the pieces of a puzzle—without laboratory studies or medical tests! Even with our advances in medicine, today's doctors still use much the same approach in diagnosing any disorder, including bipolar disorder.

The health professional's first step is to take a history of your illness. That means gathering information from you and possibly others who know you well. The second step is doing a physical examination, including a psychiatric exam that includes making systemized observations. The third step is putting the findings together to develop an accurate diagnosis.

Type I Diabetes Mellitus is an example of a syndrome that has been known for centuries. In fact, diabetes means *passing through* and refers to frequent urination, while mellitus means *honeysweet*. Young people with Type I Diabetes display symptoms of rapid weight loss, frequent thirst and frequent urination. When examined, they show physical weakness and are very ill. For centuries, physicians collected these and other symptoms and observations to identify the syndrome of diabetes. Prior to modern-day medicine, they confirmed the diagnosis by tasting the patient's urine and finding it to be sweet. That became the lab test for diabetes mellitus: tasting the urine for the sweetness caused by elevated sugars in the urine. Today, we have sophisticated laboratory tests to confirm the diagnosis of diseases like diabetes.

Laboratory Tests

Yesterday's doctors did not wait for laboratory tests to accurately diagnose diabetes mellitus. Even today, health care professionals use the results of medical tests mostly to confirm diagnoses, not to make them.

Many people with bipolar disorder ask about PET scans and blood tests for confirmation. A PET (Positive Emission Tomography) scan of the brain shows a picture of the brain's activity. It is used as a research tool and to advance knowledge of neurobiological disorders. While special tests are sometimes used in research, no lab test is available at this time to confirm the diagnosis of bipolar disorder.

The fact that specific laboratory tests are not available to diagnose bipolar disorder bothers some people, even causing them to deny the disorder exists. However, as with diabetes and thousands of other medical and psychiatric disorders, bipolar disorder has been carefully diagnosed for centuries, long before the modern concept of laboratory tests.

Since bipolar disorder is classified as a syndrome, we rely on two basic components to confirm its diagnosis. The first includes symptoms that a person reports (such as depressed mood, poor sleep or difficulty concentrating). The second is observations made by doctors and other mental health clinicians (psychologists, clinical social workers and psychiatric nurse practitioners). Mental health clinicians and primary care providers, including family doctors, physicians assistants and nurse practitioners, often refer their patients to a psychiatrist either to confirm or treat a suspected diagnosis of bipolar disorder.

The skilled clinician may notice a patient appears to be depressed, talks rapidly, can't sit still or cries easily. These symptoms are noted and additional material collected, such as family history of illness. These pieces of the puzzle are then put together until enough of the picture emerges to make a diagnosis.

Individuals with the disorder may only see some of the pieces of the puzzle. People close to them may see other pieces and provide valuable information. Mental health clinicians recognize still other pieces by making observations.

This is not a subjective task open to a lot of speculation. The facts are gathered carefully. Skilled clinicians have honed the art of recognizing and assembling data to reveal the picture that leads to a diagnosis. They use pertinent questions to help them see the long-term picture with as many pieces of the puzzle as possible. You can help assure an accurate diagnosis by sharing information honestly and by allowing those who know you best to be a part of the process.

Unfortunately, not all doctors and clinicians have been trained in diagnosing bipolar disorder. If you question your diagnosis, talk to your doctor or clinician and ask for a referral for a second opinion if you feel it is needed. Most will not feel offended by your request because they too want the very best outcome for you.

TWO DIAGNOSTIC TOOLS

To reach a diagnosis, clinicians use these two important tools: *Diagnostic and Statistical Manual of Psychiatric Disorders* (DSM) and *International Classification of Disease* (ICD). The DSM, published by the American Psychiatric Association, defines symptoms and signs of psychiatric disorders as well as specific criteria for making diagnoses. (A symptom is what a patient reports; a sign is what a clinician observes.) First published in 1952, the DSM represents a significant body of knowledge about diagnosing neurobiologic disorders in addition to brain-related emotional and genetic disorders. It has gone through a number of revisions, with DSM IV-TR (4th edition-transitional revision) currently available.

The *International Classification of Disease* (ICD), published by the World Health Organization, also describes neurobiologic disorders. Currently in its tenth revision, ICD will become more important as Medicare and other insurance providers require a switch to the ICD classification system for coding diagnoses.

THREE DIAGNOSTIC SKILLS

Clinicians use three main clinical skills for diagnosing bipolar disorder: thorough gathering of patient history, observation and the art of putting information together to see the whole.

Patient history

The first clinical skill involves obtaining a thorough history from a patient. This means a skilled clinician asks about symptoms and areas that may cause conflict or stress. Questions about your medical history are helpful, including these: Have you had episodes of depression in the past? Have you ever been hospitalized? Have you ever attempted suicide? Have you ever been diagnosed as having mania? The medical history also includes questions about medical conditions such as thyroid disease, diabetes and heart disease.

In addition, patient history involves learning about your family's medical history. Has a blood relative been diagnosed with a psychiatric disorder or other medical disorder? Is there a family history of suicide? Are there any illnesses such as thyroid disease in the family? A review of systems lists symptoms you may be having and asks about colds, cough, fatigue, chest pain, fluttering in your chest and so on.

A social history involves lifestyle questions: Do you smoke, drink, use drugs or herbal medicines? Are you single or in a relationship? Whom does your family consist of? Are you working, attending school, staying at home or not working because of physical disabilities? Knowing this information coupled with your medical history helps the clinician put the puzzle pieces together to make an accurate diagnosis.

Observation

The clinician notes these questions without asking them specifically: Do you appear sad? Are you tearful? How do you hold your body? Are you slowed down? Do you say you are happy but your face, tone of voice and body language give a different message? These observations and more can help a well-trained clinician determine whether depression is your diagnosis.

Are you talking rapidly, having difficulty focusing or are you constantly in motion? Do you dress in a wildly flamboyant way? Do you express grandiose thoughts? If some of the answers are yes, these puzzle pieces tip off the clinician that mania may be your diagnosis.

Then the clinician puts all the information together to form a picture, similar to how detectives gather clues and patiently piece them together to reconstruct how a crime happened. The more clues they gather, the easier it is to "see" the whole scenario. But even with all the clues in the world, the detectives still have to make that final leap of "seeing" the entire picture. Like detectives, clinicians learn to analyze "clues" through their experience and training.

The art of seeing the whole picture

At this point, the clinician weighs the diagnosis of bipolar disorder against other possible diagnoses that have similar features and then considers questions like these: Could medicines you take cause some of your symptoms? Is a chronic illness present? Are you using street drugs or alcohol? Are you grieving a significant loss? Is there a pattern of depression in your family that suggests a possible genetic component? Are you under an unusual amount of stress causing an emotional overload that has contributed to depression?

In some cases, clinicians ask for specific medical tests like drawing some blood for a thyroid test and others tests that can rule out a medical illness causing the symptoms.

Then they put all of the information together to form a picture, just as detectives gather clues to determine what really happened. The more clues they gather, the easier it is to get a clear idea of the overall picture. And the clearer the picture, the more accurate the diagnosis.

Caution about self-diagnosis

You can read about the diagnostic process for bipolar disorder in the Diagnostic and Statistical Manual of Psychiatric Disorders. (Use the acrostic DSM when you do an electronic search; this combination of letters will yield more results than the full title.) I encourage you to study books and articles or use the Internet if you are interested in the diagnostic process for bipolar disorder.

Remember, though, it takes far more than reading to diagnose any disorder accurately. No matter how much you read, you will not gain the skills necessary to diagnose yourself. Even if you have specific training and experience, you still need a skilled, objective clinician to diagnose any condition you may have.

SUMMARY

Bipolar disorder is a syndrome. Diagnosis requires gathering symptoms and making observations. These form the puzzle pieces of bipolar disorder. To make a diagnosis the puzzle pieces have to come together to reveal the whole picture.

Next we will learn about treatments for bipolar disorder.

Treatments for Bipolar Disorder

GETTING TREATMENT for bipolar disorder has proven to work effectively; avoiding treatment can lead to low productivity, disability, social problems and even death. *You have every reason to believe your life will improve with proper treatment* because treatment decreases the number of episodes of depression and mania and helps you get on track. It is never too late to get back on track. Even if your disorder does not seem severe at this moment, treatment still improves life and may prevent this illness from getting worse. So the sooner you get appropriate treatment, the sooner you will improve. Treatment works and it is essential!

BECOME EXPERTS

Treatment for bipolar disorder has three major components. The first is education about the disorder itself, the second is psychotherapy and the third is medical therapy. Education is important because the best thing for you and those you care about is to become experts about the disorder. Learn about its symptoms and the triggers that make it worse. Also learn about treating and managing the disorder so you can live well with the challenges of bipolar disorder.

This is true not only for this disorder but for any disorder that is chronic or recurrent. A chronic disorder lasts for years or for a lifetime. A recurring disorder takes vacations at times, but there is always a possibility that it will come back home to flare up right in the middle of things.

People who have diabetes also need to learn to manage their disease and master living with it. Their mastery involves learning about foods, exercise and adjusting medications.

"As a person experiencing bipolar disorder, you can become a master of the world of mood!" (Ann Terrill-Torrez). Learning can come in many ways. Your doctor or therapist will help you, but you can add to your knowledge by reading books like this one. The Recovery Resources section (pp 141-143) will give you some guidance on books I have found to be helpful. There are new books coming out all the time, so ask your librarian or local bookseller to help you find as much information as you can.

If you have access to the Internet, search for information that helps you learn more. Your doctor or therapist may also be able to direct you to classes in the community and can provide education as a part of your treatment.

Becoming educated also means talking with others to learn how they live with this challenging disorder. Be on the lookout for therapies that may not be readily available to you. Perhaps your therapist is excellent and helps you make good progress but is not trained or experienced in more recent therapies that also work. If you identify a therapy that you think will be helpful, talk it over with your therapist and decide together if it is appropriate to incorporate it into your therapy.

MEDICAL TREATMENTS

In addition to psychotherapy, medical treatments such as taking medications have been found to be enormously effective in treating bipolar disorder. In fact, using medications is considered by many to be the most important form of treatment. However, because medications are so effective, some people get the idea that education and psychotherapy are not necessary in the treatment of bipolar disorder. In my opinion, you wouldn't want to miss out on anything that can help you feel better.

PSYCHOTHERAPY

Reading this book will help you learn more about the world of moods. But when you're in therapy, you have an objective, highly trained person who will help you sort out what is important for you at a particular time.

Psychotherapy is essential in feeling the best you can. There are a lot of psychotherapy jokes out there, and the media often portray psychotherapy as a negative experience. Many have the idea that in psychotherapy people rehash every little thing that happened as a child or that they're going to lie on a couch and speak thoughts that come in a free fall pattern.

Enter the 21st century! Today, there are effective, well-tested psychotherapies for bipolar disorder. They work! Here we learn about some of them that have proven effectiveness, but this will just be scratching the surface of what is helping people live well with bipolar disorder. For now the message is to stay in therapy and take responsibility for learning to manage bipolar disorder using every kind of help that's available.

Your therapist may choose to use different settings that will help you in different ways. For instance, perhaps your therapist will want those close to you to be involved in family therapy. Remember, families are not always traditional. Family therapy can involve those who are close to you, not just "family" in the stereotyped form of a man and a woman and 2.4 children.

At other times, it will be most helpful for you and your therapist to work together without anyone else present. Therapy classes are also effective, especially for education. In classes, you will learn from others who experience some of the same challenges you experience. Interaction with other people presents a different perspective that can help you learn skills to live well.

Therapy may follow a wide range of structures. In some cases, it is more directed than others. For example, you may work with your therapist on a selected topic such as interpersonal relationships, and treatment may consist of a certain number of sessions focusing on just this issue. In other cases, therapy may be more flexible and bring in many different aspects of life at any given session.

Many of the topics you will address in therapy are common to everyone. They include challenges in relationships, life styles and ways of thinking. The challenges of living with extremes of mood can make these everyday challenges difficult to manage. With or without bipolar disorder, difficulties in relationships and difficulties with problem solving can be areas that need attention. Other challenges can include learning to stabilize routines or deal with symptoms of poor sleep. Management skills for irritability can be extremely useful.

Some people have difficulty meeting deadlines for school

or work. This can be amplified by periods of not feeling well or by necessary hospitalizations. Finding a balance in life activities can be challenging for anybody, but extremes of mood can make this balancing act even more difficult.

As I said before, there are many excellent therapies for bipolar disorder. Some are basic therapies that have been around for years. Others are newer therapies specific to bipolar disorder or ones that have been adapted to address issues specific to bipolar disorder. While it is impossible to review all the possible therapies, some have been found to be especially effective in treatment of bipolar disorder. They are described below.

If your therapist doesn't use these particular therapies, that doesn't mean your work together will be ineffective. Learn the principles of each therapy and apply some of these to your own recovery journey. Discuss them with your therapist if you have difficulty seeing the connection to your own situation.

1. Interpersonal Social Rhythm Therapy (IPSRT)—developed by Ellen Frank and others.

When relationships with others are shored up, there is a foundation for improved mental health. This therapy recognizes that relationships change with a diagnosis of bipolar disorder. I have found this to be true in my own life, with the loss of many friends directly due to bipolar disorder.

When this happened some of my friends did not know how to be supportive. Most of my friends would have helped me if I had been able to ask for what I needed. Therapies such as IPSRT can help you learn skills to foster healthy relationships or to terminate relationships when necessary.

IPSRT also deals with the grief that is a common result of having any kind of chronic illness. When we lose our "healthy self," we have a difficult job to grieve our loss and to get in touch with the part of us that we truly are, in spite of the effects of bipolar disorder. We need to come to terms with the fact that bipolar disorder is just one small part of who we are. Too often we take on the role of being "bipolar" and lose track of the fact that we are also teachers, engineers, brothers or sisters, musicians, gardeners, grandparents—you name it, we all have other identities besides those connected with bipolar disorder!

Even in recognizing these other identities and managing to keep them strong, there can still be an experience of alarming grief over the loss of "healthy self." Our life roles can change, often without our permission, and the resultant tailspin can be addressed in psychotherapy.

IPSRT recognizes the impact bipolar disorder has on our biologic rhythms. Biologic rhythms include our body's regulation of sleep patterns, energy levels and appetite. The brain regulates biologic rhythms through hormones and other messengers to our body. Keeping our daily routines stable has been shown to have a positive impact on our biologic rhythms.

In bipolar disorder, biologic rhythms take on a life of their own. Our biologic rhythms can cause us to wake up at any time. Our energy levels fluctuate without warning. Our appetite is hard to predict. We can help stabilize these biologic rhythms by maintaining a consistent routine. In my case, I find that going to bed and getting up at the same time each day helps me manage the symptoms of bipolar disorder. I take control of other activities as well, avoiding over-stimulation that can feed mania or under-stimulation that can prolong depression.

IPSRT helps you identify activities that are out of balance in your life. It encourages you to gradually rein them in one by one so you can stabilize daily rhythms. In turn, this stabilization has a positive effect on your biologic rhythms. The result is feeling better because biologic rhythms are disrupted less severely by the effects of bipolar disorder.

2. *Cognitive Behavioral Therapy* (CBT)—*developed by Cory F. Newman and others.*

CBT is a therapy that helps you consider the impact of thinking style on mood. It helps you change patterns that contribute to mood difficulties.

CBT identifies automatic ways of thinking that fuel depression and behaviors that energize mania. CBT has been around for decades in the treatment of depression. During the past decade, it has been used in mania as well.

In depression, thoughts such as putting oneself down or believing that plans will not work out are commonly identified. With CBT you can learn to refute these thoughts and replace them with alternate ways of thinking that will increase your confidence and help you face daily challenges.

With mania, the strategies of CBT are slightly different. They focus more on checking out your ideas with others rather than acting on strong feelings leading to counterproductive behaviors. The management skill of delaying actions is also effective. For example, I have found at times when I experience symptoms of mania that I want to take on several projects at once. Waiting to consult with others who know me best can keep me from making too many commitments—a situation that might energize mania to a point that I become more and more irritable and disorganized.

3. *Family Focused Therapy (FFT)—developed by David Miklowitz.*

FFT is a therapy that was developed in the context of hospitalization of a family member because of bipolar disorder. It's helpful to address the impact of bipolar disorder on the family. FFT, however, does not make bipolar disorder the center of attention. Instead, it helps families learn to examine relational patterns in order to build stronger alliances within the structure of the family.

FFT teaches communication skills and uses role-playing to help families buff up their problem-solving skills. It acknowledges the emotionally laden issues that sometimes remain hidden in a family's daily interactions and teaches families to acknowledge and deal with them. Shoring up the family's skills of identifying challenges and actively finding solutions together decreases hospitalizations and in addition increases the time between episodes of severe symptoms of bipolar disorder.

Summary

This chapter described examples of psychotherapy applied specifically to bipolar disorder. Not all will be best for you at any given time. It is important that you talk with your therapist and doctor while seeking the best treatment for bipolar disorder.

Remember, there is a distinct body of knowledge and skills to learn in order to master the world of mood. Medical treatments will next be described in more detail.

Medical Treatments

PRESCRIPTION MEDICATION

OFTEN WHEN first diagnosed with bipolar disorder, people feel reluctant to take medications and, later, to stay on medications. It's never the highlight of the day! In addition, we live in a society in which there is considerable ambivalence about taking medications. Despite the pros and cons to taking them, some people will reject them without considering the facts. Or people might stop taking them for logical reasons but fail to consider the entire picture.

If taking medication is an issue with you, this chapter will add some big-picture highlights you may not have considered. Please use this information as a jumping-off point for further discussion with your doctor, not as medical advice.

Research has shown that medications are extremely effective in the treatment of bipolar disorder. Stabilizing mood through medication is a powerful tool in the treatment of bipolar disorder. According to studies, cycling back and forth from mania to depression is decreased with the help of medications and the affected person will have fewer mood swings over a lifetime.

For those who feel euphoric when they experience mania, this may not sound like a good thing. Who wants to trade euphoria for stability? But considering the bigger picture, one must remember that the *eu*phoria of mania is followed by the *dys*phoria of depression. Productivity and creativity may seem to be a benefit of mania, but in the long run, having a stable mood produces a more consistent pattern of accomplishment. Mood stability enables people to take control of their lives instead of being controlled by swings of mania and depression.

TAKING MEDICATION REGULARLY

So why not just take medication when your mood is unstable or you're feeling bad?

One answer is that taking medications all the time will result in far greater mood stability over your lifetime. In addition, mood instability is accompanied by difficulties personally and socially, in relationships at work and outside of it.

Remember the characteristics of bipolar disorder discussed in the previous chapter? A spree that results from mania can destroy your finances. A deep depression can decrease your productivity or isolate you from daily activities. The emotional pain from untreated bipolar disorder can devastate you, your family and friends. Other potential risks include disability, unnecessary hospitalization—even death by suicide.

Second, medications require time to take effect. It can take several weeks and even several months for a medicine to work effectively. It's sometimes hard to recognize when an episode of depression or mania is beginning, so it would be difficult to recognize when to restart medicine to prevent a recurrence.

ONE SIZE DOES NOT FIT ALL

Realize that medicines are not quick fixes. The fantasy that "popping" pills will cure mental disorders is just that—a fantasy. Rather, pills can help you take control of your chronic illness. Though we have many effective medicines for treating bipolar disorder, there is no wonder-drug and one size does not fit all. Thus, it is important to understand that the first medicine tried isn't always the best for a particular individual. A great deal of patience is required. Often it takes several tries for your doctor to figure out what will work. In the future, scientists should be able to identify some genetic clues to guide doctors' selection of medication with the help of a simple blood test.

SEVERAL MEDICATIONS NEEDED

Most people with bipolar disorder require two or even several medications in combination to enable them to have the best control of the disorder. Adding one medicine on top of another can change how they both work. That means treatment can be more effective by using more than one medicine. The challenging part is to be able to balance the side effects of medications. The benefit of taking charge of bipolar disorder and leading a satisfying life outweighs the risk of side effects for most people.

All medications have a long list of possible side effects. Even taking a placebo pill that has no active medicine will cause side effects. (Placebos, by the way, are used in research only, not in clinical practice. When they are used in research trials, the subject is always told that the use of placebos is part of the trial.)

Report side effects to your prescriber so you can decide together whether the side effects are tolerable or intolerable. If they are intolerable, you may need to try another medication.

Simply changing the dosage or taking the medication differently can often treat side effects. Some side effects go away altogether after a short time on the medicine. Adding a second medication can easily treat some side effects. This may sound like adding more trouble, but if a medicine is working well for you, you may not want to take the risk of exchanging it for another one that does not work as well.

Though it is rare, side effects can be dangerous and may require you to stop taking the medication immediately. Your prescriber will tell you in advance what side effects to report immediately and pharmacies also provide written instructions when prescriptions are filled. Report any side effects as accurately as possible to your doctor so you can decide together whether a change is needed.

MEDICATIONS AND ADDICTION

Some people do not want to take medicines because they make associations between medicines and street drugs. Our society makes a massive effort to educate people about the dangers of addiction. As a family physician, I have heard many patients say they don't want to be on medicine because they are afraid of becoming addicted or that medicines will lose their effects if taken for too long a period.

Most of the medications prescribed for bipolar disorder will not cause addiction. However, your doctor may recommend a medication that could potentially become addicting. If this happens, it is important to understand the difference between *dependence* and *addiction*. Medicines known as "addictive" are actually ones that cause dependence. If you become dependent on a medication, the medicine cannot be stopped suddenly without causing symptoms of withdrawal. Remember, dependence is not addiction. An addiction requires a psychological need for that medication and leads to behaviors like pushing to get dosages increased or getting the same prescriptions from different doctors at the same time.

If you have bipolar disorder and already have an addiction disorder, it is wise to tell your doctor about the addiction before taking a medicine that could lead to a further addiction problem. Choose a different medicine that does not have the potential of causing dependence.

ISSUES OF STOPPING MEDICATION

When stopping most medications used for bipolar disorder, a slow taper is often best unless there is a specific reason that requires rapid discontinuation. It is always wise to consult with your doctor if you think you need to stop a medicine. You may think your medication isn't working so you want to stop taking it. This may be especially true for some medications you have taken for less than three months. Consult with your doctor before taking action; you may not have been on your medication long enough to see its benefits.

Medications are expensive and you may think that you can get by without taking them all the time in order to save money. Weigh this against the possibility of missed days of work, the loss of a job or an unnecessary hospitalization. If you are having trouble paying for your medications, you may be eligible for medication programs in your community. Many manufacturers also have programs for people who cannot afford their medications.

Ask your psychiatrist and family doctor for details. If they can't assist you, call your nearest medical school, your local college's social work department, your Mental Health Association, your state health department or The United Way. Help is usually available but requires persistence to track it down. If you have difficulty persisting on your own, ask a family member or friend to help you.

CREATIVITY & MEDICATION

Often I hear people say that they fear treatment for bipolar disorder will take away their creativity or change their personality. But this is not the goal of treatment. Rather, treatment helps you feel the best you can so your creativity and personality can remain valuable assets in your life. These qualities require stability of mood for productive expression. An example is author Virginia Woolf. In the extreme moods of her illness, she wrote nothing. Her creativity, rather than being augmented by illness, was squelched. When she was experiencing relative stability of mood, she was able to write her best works.

OTHER THERAPIES

Besides treatment with medications, medical management for bipolar disorder may include other treatments such as full spectrum light therapy, electroconvulsive treatment (ECT) and diet.

Light therapy

With light therapy, you simply sit in front of a light box that delivers full spectrum light. Light therapy acts as an antidepressant and should not be tried without a prescription. The amount of light and length of time under the light is significant since inappropriate amounts of light can destabilize mood rather than help it.

Electroconvulsive therapy (ECT)

ECT, sometimes called "shock" therapy, is not done in the way most movies portray it. It is an effective, safe and sometimes life-saving treatment when used in certain circumstances. It is actually safer and works more rapidly than medications for some individuals, especially for those who may be on medications for other medical conditions. It is also effective in elders with certain medical conditions that make taking medications for bipolar disorder unsafe. Those who cannot tolerate medications for bipolar disorder may also benefit from ECT.

If you doctor suggests ECT, take time to learn about it. Ask questions about the process and possible side effects such as difficulties with memory.

Diet

Ongoing research into the role of diet in the treatment of bipolar disorder may produce effective treatments. Some have been helped by the addition of omega three fatty acids. Others have found that certain foods or substances may trigger episodes of depression or mania. If learning more interests you, ask your doctor to refer you to a nutritionist who has knowledge of diet and its effects on bipolar disorder.

SUMMARY

This chapter has reviewed some of the pros and cons of taking medication. You will want to balance risks and benefits when you weigh your doctor's advice about medications. When you are on a medication, it is important to discuss side effects and take medications as directed. If you want to stop a medication, talk to your doctor first. Learn about your medicines so you can feel comfortable taking them. Additional medical treatments were also discussed.

The next chapter will answer some important questions about medicines and how they are used in the treatment of bipolar disorder.

Types of Medication

WHEN I was practicing family medicine, I had to know how hundreds of medications worked and interacted. Professionals who prescribe medications think of them in groups first, then as individual medications within sub-groups. These groups and their sub-groups are called "classes."

A class of medication is often defined by its primary usage. For instance, the class called antidepressants has as its primary use the treatment of depression. Antidepressants can also be used for treating anxiety, muscle tension and incontinence.

It's like thinking about cars and trucks. We all recognize the general classes of coupes, four-doors, pick-up trucks and semis. We know that they have different uses with some overlap. For instance, my husband and I used to own a car that had a hatch-back. When the back seat was up, it could carry people; when it was down, we could carry larger items and use it like a truck.

Medicines are much the same in that we can divide them into classes and use them for different purposes. Usually classes of medications are defined by the way they work, by what they do or perhaps by what they were first used for. For example, medicines for blood pressure are in the large class of antihypertensives; that is, they treat high blood pressure in order to prevent long-term complications.

Antihypertensives are further divided into smaller groups according to the way they work. One group or class of antihypertensives works on the kidneys, another class on the blood vessels and so on. Medicines in the larger class of antihypertensives are also used to treat diseases other than high blood pressure, including treating heart disease, kidney disease, even baldness and prostate problems.

Just as I could use my hatchback to carry larger items instead of people, an anti-hypertensive medicine can be used for disorders other than high blood pressure. When the Food and Drug Administration (FDA) approves a medicine, it approves it for a specific "indication." An indication means the use of a specific medication for a specific purpose. A medicine can only be marketed for indications for which the FDA has approved it. For example, an anti-hypertensive medicine may be approved with an indication for use in high blood pressure.

This is why you may pick up your medicine for bipolar disorder and discover the pharmacist's instructions say the medicine is for seizure disorders. Many medicines for seizure disorders treat bipolar disorder but some do not yet have FDA approval for bipolar disorder. If you have any questions about why a medicine is being used for bipolar disorder, be sure to ask your doctor or pharmacist.

Several classes of medications are commonly used for bipolar disorder. It is helpful to know the class to which your medicines belong so you can understand why you are on a certain medication. It also helps you know about possible side effects and different ways the medicines are used.

MOOD STABILIZERS

The so-called "first-line" medicines used in bipolar disorder over the past several decades have been in a large class called mood stabilizers. "First-line" means that a medicine in a class is most often chosen first for a specific condition.

Nearly everyone with bipolar disorder who takes medicine will be on a mood stabilizer. As noted earlier, someone with bipolar disorder has the inability to consistently regulate mood within a normal range. Since this inability to regulate mood within a normal range is at the core of the disorder, the first step is to stabilize mood so you do not feel like you are swinging back and forth from mania to depression.

Besides stabilizing moods, a mood stabilizer also has a preventive effect because it helps prevent mood swings in the future. Continuing on a mood stabilizer even though your mood is stable will help prevent future recurrences of mood instability.

For many, it is difficult to understand the necessity of staying on the medicine even when feeling better. Think about taking an antibiotic for an infection; you usually take it for a short time. But when you have a chronic and recurring disorder such as bipolar disorder, your medicine helps you feel better long term. Thus, it is best to stay on a medicine even when you are feeling well.

In a way, treatment for bipolar disorder is like treatment for diabetes. Someone with diabetes requiring insulin will feel better after blood sugars are controlled. However, if insulin is stopped, a relapse will occur rapidly. It is easy to see that continuing insulin therapy is necessary.

With bipolar disorder the need to continue medicine may not be as easily recognized. This is because failing to take prescribed medicine may not result in an immediate return of symptoms. It is easier to believe that feeling better will last even without medicine. Unfortunately this is not the case, and without medicine the relapse rate is high.

Just as my hatchback did more than carry people in the backseat, so mood stabilizers may do more than stabilize mood. Besides making mood more even, they may treat mania or depression or help you sleep better. In some cases, sleeping better comes as a side effect (a good one to have when sleep eludes you).

Under the general class of mood stabilizers, there are several sub-classes. In this section, we talk about the subclasses but not individual medications. Remember, new medications are coming out all the time. You can learn about them from your doctor, your therapist and your pharmacist.

Lithium

The first sub-class of mood stabilizers is made up of only one medicine, a salt called lithium. For a long time, lithium was the only mood stabilizer available. Extremely effective for many, it is widely used to treat bipolar disorder. Because it is a salt, it can cause thirst, frequent urination and water retention.

Antiseizure

The next sub-class of mood stabilizers is that of antiseizure medications. Do not be confused. If people with bipolar disorder have seizures, it is a coincidence. But some antiseizure medications have the capability to stabilize mood and they have an indication or approval to be used in treating bipolar disorder. Besides stabilizing mood, many have an antidepressant effect. They can be given at bedtime to help with sleep because they often have the side effect of sedation.

Antipsychotics

A third sub-class of mood stabilizers is made up of antipsychotics, some of which are now approved by the FDA for bipolar disorder. This class of medications is being used more and more along with other mood stabilizers to treat bipolar disorder. (Antipsychotics also make up a class of their own and are covered separately on page 94.)

Antihypertensives

Some consider a fourth group of mood stabilizers to be calcium channel blockers. These medicines are actually in the class of antihypertensives used to treat high blood pressure and heart disease. They work on "calcium channels." Calcium channels are found throughout the cells of the body and in brain cells.

However, in a person with high blood pressure and certain other medical problems, they might be considered for treating both hypertension and bipolar disorder along with other medications for bipolar disorder. In addition, if other mood stabilizers are ineffective, it may be worth trying a calcium channel blocker if your doctor recommends one.

ANTIDEPRESSANTS

This class of medicines is used to treat and prevent episodes of depression. Many antidepressants can also be used to help with sleep.

Often antidepressants are not added to a person's medicines until the mood has first been stabilized with a mood stabilizer. This is because in the absence of a mood stabilizer, there is a danger that antidepressants will cause either mania or rapid cycling.

When you are on an antidepressant, it is important to help your prescriber monitor your mood. When an antidepressant or any medication is added to your medicines, it is especially important to keep all of your appointments, communicate your moods and report any return of symptoms you usually have when you experience mania.

As with mood stabilizers, antidepressants are sometimes chosen for their side effects as well as their specific benefits. Many of the antidepressants help with sleep and some are more activating than others, that is, they give you more energy. In addition, other medical conditions may be taken into account. Migraine headaches, chronic pain, muscle spasm and urinary incontinence are all conditions treated with antidepressants.

Desire to get moving

Once when I was on an antidepressant soon after I had been diagnosed with bipolar disorder, I wanted to get more motion into my life. In fact, I acted on this by riding my bike on a bike trail that runs along a river. Even now this seems like one of the most wonderful times I have ever had. It was characterized by an expansive mood in which I enjoyed not only my own boundless energy but also the energy of the flow of the river.

Today, I readily recognize this as a symptom of mania that should have been reported to my doctor. At the time, though, it seemed so natural to me that I didn't report it. It took a couple of extra weeks before we were able to ascertain that I was experiencing mania induced by the antidepressant I was taking. If we had stopped the medicine sooner, I might have done better in the long haul.

ANTIPSYCHOTICS

Antipsychotics can help with the psychotic symptoms that frequently accompany bipolar disorder. They can also help with sleep or agitation. Thus, your doctor may add an antipsychotic to your medicines even if you don't have psychotic symptoms.

Often individuals believe that taking an antipsychotic is frightening because they think of psychosis as being a scary thing. It is easy to think of oneself as sicker when an antipsychotic is added to one's medicine. It is more helpful, however, to view such an addition as treating an unwanted symptom, augmenting the effect of a mood stabilizer or treating the extremes of mood of bipolar disorder.

BENZODIAZEPINES

These are used for sleep, agitation or anxiety. They may be used on a regular basis or only as needed. For example, to treat agitation that occurs as infrequently as once or twice a week, a benzodiazepine may be prescribed to take only at those times. Because the benzodiazepines can cause dependence, they may not be suggested for those with a substance or dependence disorder.

If you have a diagnosis of bipolar disorder and an addictive disorder of any kind, your decision to begin a potentially addictive medication needs serious consideration. It must be done only with extreme caution and after a thorough discussion with your doctor. In fact, in most cases your doctor will probably choose other medicines instead. The risk may very well be too high to even consider this class of medication.

Benzodiazepines can affect your thinking process and slow down your ability to process information. This is true of other classes of medicines used to treat bipolar disorder and it is true of the disorder itself. If you are having such problems, discuss them with your doctor.

HYPNOTICS

Hypnotics have nothing to do with hypnosis. They are often called "sleepers" because they help with sleep problems. There are a number of hypnotics available but many are approved for short-term use only. Still, they may be useful.

Most of the medicines mentioned in this chapter can help with sleep problems. For some individuals, the side effect of drowsiness makes them good for promoting sleep. The side effect of drowsiness of the older antihistamines can be used for sleep. Some of these may be bought over the counter, so be sure to ask you doctor first before trying one of them.

Coming out of depression: Danger!

*Your doctor watches for what happens to your actions when you come out of a severe depression. You may have been suicidal but not have the energy to pull it off. Being put on an antidepressant may bump you up toward a more normal mood, giving you more energy. If the suicidal thoughts do not resolve quickly, you may still be suicidal, but now you have enough energy to **act** on your thoughts. This is why it is important to be on a mood stabilizer along with the antidepressant. It will be less likely that you will hit that dangerous combination of feeling suicidal and having the energy to act on it. If you observe this combination of feeling suicidal and having the energy to take action, get help right away.*

OTHER MEDICATIONS

Stimulants are rarely used for the treatment of bipolar disorder. Medicines used for Alzheimer patients can also be tried if an individual with bipolar is having difficulty processing information or remembering things.

Herbal Remedies

If you choose to take herbal remedies, be sure to consult with a highly trained expert in the field. More medical doctors are getting this type of training, yet they are still hard to find. Remember that doctors study for a minimum of seven years to become Board Certified. They take multiple exams and go through an extensive licensing process.

Herbologists also study for an equivalent time if they are well trained. Unfortunately, you can walk into a health food store and receive advice from an untrained sales clerk who looks for information in a book or from a fellow clerk. What's more, some think that the word "natural" or "organic" means that the product is safe to use and somehow better than a prescription.

Over-the-counter herbal medicines are not regulated by the federal government as prescription medicines are. Many of these products do not contain standard amounts of the herbal preparation being advertised. Some herbal medicines can make bipolar disorder worse and others can interact with the medicines you are taking. If you choose to use these products, be sure to seek out good medical advice and discuss this with your psychiatrist.

SUMMARY

In this chapter we discussed the various classes of medications and how they might work together. We also briefly addressed herbal remedies.

Next we will discover issues of substance abuse as they relate to bipolar disorder.

Mixing Bipolar with Substance Abuse

YOU MAY want to skip this chapter if you don't abuse substances of any kind, or if you use them but aren't addicted to them. However, even if this is true, I recommend you learn about this topic because it's important to understand the connection between bipolar disorder and substance abuse. Some studies show that as many as 60% of people with bipolar disorder also have some form of substance abuse disorder. Compare this to the general population that has a 15% rate of substance abuse.

Two Disorders Coexist

Bipolar disorder and substance abuse disorders have what is called a high comorbidity. That means the two disorders often coexist in one person. In fact, not only can both disorders coexist, they may even make each other worse.

Even if you've never used addictive substances, or if you used them in the distant past, understand the close link between bipolar disorder and substance abuse so you can make healthier choices. For instance, when I was a teenager, I knew that there was alcoholism in my extended family. I decided not to risk experiencing alcohol addiction by choosing not to drink alcohol. Although at the time I was unaware that I had bipolar disorder, my current understanding of the connection between bipolar disorder and substance abuse makes me thankful that I don't drink alcohol except on rare occasions.

Avoiding addictive substances can be more difficult if your background is one in which substance use is normal. You may have been exposed to appropriate, moderate use of alcohol that does not lead to abuse or addiction; this could make it difficult to imagine life without alcohol. Even today, alcohol and other drugs of addiction can seem to be an integral part of friendship and of socializing. Thus, you may not connect these substances with your experience of bipolar disorder, whether or not you have problem with addiction. In addition, you may have this challenge in your life, but are not yet ready to face it.

DUAL DIAGNOSES

Ultimately, you may know you have both an addictive disorder as well as bipolar disorder, which medically is called *dual diagnoses*. Perhaps this term seems strange since dual simply means two. By this definition, any two diagnoses such as diabetes in conjunction with bipolar disorder could be called a dual diagnoses.

However, the important word here is not *dual* but *diagnoses*. Substance abuse or addiction is a disorder that can be diagnosed and treated; it is not a character flaw or weakness. If you have both diabetes and bipolar disorder, for example, you can easily understand that both must be treated. Similarly, if you have an addiction disorder in addition to bipolar disorder, you have two different medical diagnoses. You have an addiction disorder plus a bipolar disorder. Both must be treated for you to feel better.

"War on Drugs"

In our society, addiction is seen as a societal problem. Indeed, the government has made the use of illegal drugs a criminal offence, declaring a "war on drugs." This is partly motivated for the good of our society because using drugs or alcohol can be dangerous. As an example, intoxication combined with driving frequently results in accidents and death.

However, seeing substance abuse or addiction disorders only as societal problems can ignore the fact that these are medical disorders. Instead of declaring war on other medical disorders, we need to treat them! If you have diabetes, heart disease, asthma or bipolar disorder, you can get a diagnosis and receive treatment. Similarly, if you have an abuse or addiction disorder, it can be diagnosed and successfully treated.

Substance abuse and addiction disorders frequently occur hand-in-glove with bipolar disorder and other neurobiologic disorders. We frequently hear that people with neurobiologic disorders "self-medicate" with substances of abuse. That means if you have depression, you might try to alleviate it by using alcohol. If you are experiencing mania, you may use cocaine to make the "high" last longer. These are examples of "self-medication."

But the concept of self-medication may not provide the best framework for discussing bipolar disorder combined with substance abuse and addiction disorders. It does not allow for this fact: the onset of bipolar disorder does not need to precede the onset of substance abuse/addiction. Indeed, three different things can actually happen:

1. An abuse or addictive disorder comes first and triggers the development of bipolar disorder in a person with a genetic predisposition to bipolar disorder.
2. The bipolar disorder itself increases the likelihood of a substance abuse/addiction at a later time.
3. Bipolar disorder and a substance abuse disorder begin at the same time.

UNPLEASANT SIDE

In addition, the concept of self-medication does not acknowledge the unpleasant side effects of substance abuse. For example, why would someone "self-medicate" depression with a depressant like alcohol? Alternatively, why would someone with mania use cocaine to "self-medicate" when cocaine actually prolongs and intensifies the "high" of mania? In spite of this inconsistency, these are the drugs of choice for individuals experiencing depression or mania.

Yet when we classify substance abuse separately as a treatable medical condition, we understand better the impact that substance abuse and bipolar disorder have on each other. More important, we can seek effective treatment for both disorders when they occur at the same time.

From the perspective of a family physician, if a person came to me having suffered a heart attack and also having high blood sugar from diabetes, I would never say, "I think I will treat the heart attack and postpone treatment for diabetes," or, "Let's treat the diabetes first and when it is under control, we'll treat the heart attack." Rather, I know that getting the person's blood sugar to a normal level aids in treating a heart attack. Treating the heart attack helps stabilize the diabetes. I would treat both conditions at the same time. Similarly, when an abuse or addiction disorder occurs with bipolar disorder, both need to be treated at the same time. Treatment of one results in better treatment of the other.

RECONSIDER USING ALCOHOL OR DRUGS

Clinicians prefer to treat these disorders simultaneously because the substances of abuse often interfere with the medications used to treat bipolar disorder. So whether or not you have an addiction problem, I encourage you to reconsider your use of alcohol and other drugs, even caffeine. Ask yourself these five questions:

1. Is your use of alcohol contributing to your symptoms of depression?
2. Do you become rapidly intoxicated when you use alcohol or another drug with your medications?
3. Does your use of caffeine, which is a stimulant, cause an increase in mania?
4. Do you use an addictive substance such as cocaine to increase or prolong episodes of mania?
5. Is there a relationship between your use of an addictive substance and mood swings?

If you answer "yes" to any of these questions, discuss them with your mental health clinician or primary care provider. Remember that your goal is to become healthier so you can enhance the process of recovering from bipolar disorder. If you are currently in treatment for or have a history of abuse/ addiction, be sure to tell your mental health provider. Often a person will not receive treatment for substance abuse/addiction in a psychiatric program or will not receive psychiatric treatment in a substance abuse program if the provider is not fully informed. Ideally, when both are treated simultaneously, you can achieve a level of recovery that's stable and your symptoms can be treated as they arise.

Many leading authorities believe that treatment of addiction disorders should be modified from a traditional confrontational approach. The confrontational approach can worsen bipolar disorder and lead to avoiding treatment. Consider seeking a modified approach when you are exploring treatment options for a substance abuse program.

COMMUNITY RECOVERY GROUPS

Besides abandoning addictive substances, you can enhance your recovery by attending community recovery groups. One group that addresses both addiction disorders and bipolar disorder is Double Trouble in Recovery. Call your local Mental Health Association, National Alliance for the Mentally Ill (NAMI), your local Mental Health Center or The United Way for more information. You can also search the Internet. These and other resources are listed in the Recovery Resources section at the end of this book (pp 141-143).

Alcoholics Anonymous, Cocaine Anonymous and Narcotics Anonymous provide other avenues of support and have groups in most cities. Remember, these groups will focus on addiction. The other "half" of your dual diagnosis, bipolar disorder, may not even be mentioned. If you can successfully get addiction challenges under control but continue to experience symptoms of bipolar disorder, focus on treatment for bipolar disorder. At the same time, recognize that symptoms of addiction still need to be addressed when they arise. Both disorders need to be treated with equal vigor.

YOUR FAMILY'S CONCERN

It is important to talk with your family when bipolar disorder and abuse or addiction diagnoses occur together. Your significant other should learn how to support you in ways that don't encourage substance abuse. Often when family members lack education and understanding of addiction disorders, they inadvertently enable your continued use of addictive substances. Groups such as Al-Anon can provide education and support for your family.

Also, be sure to talk to your children (if you have them) about the link between addiction disorders and bipolar disorder. Educate yourself and your family about the risks of addiction for a person who has bipolar disorder and be aware that your biological children share much of your genetic make-up. Because of this, they have an increased risk for both addiction disorders and bipolar disorder. It's up to you to inform them they may have a greater risk of developing these disorders compared with their friends, for example.

AWARENESS OF RISKS

Always carefully weigh the risks you take by using addictive substances such as alcohol in combination with your medications. Talk to your doctor if you haven't already, to determine an appropriate use of alcohol. Also, plan ways to recognize increased use or signs of substance abuse. Remember that major life events such as a loss or separation, a move to a new location, or a flare-up of bipolar disorder, can trigger the onset of an addictive disorder. Likewise, positive experiences such as a promotion or new child at home can trigger an onset because of increased stress.

Most important, because of the high co-existence of bipolar disorder and addiction disorders, consider abstaining from the use of all addictive substances. Why? Because alcohol or street drugs may change the way medicine works in your body. Be sure to talk to your doctor or therapist about any use of addictive substances. They want to help, not judge.

If you experience bipolar disorder, this conversation absolutely must take place. The extremely high rate of dual diagnoses (as high as 60%) means you carry a high risk of having an addiction disorder. If you choose stop taking addictive substances but have difficulty stopping, ask for help. Be persistent, because addressing this issue will pay off with good health.

Modulating Moods

T HE TERM bipolar can be confusing when we compare its literal meaning with the disorder it describes. *Bi* means two and *polar* refers to extremes or poles. Hearing the term *bipolar,* you may imagine something that has no resemblance to your experience with the disorder. In fact, bipolar disorder is often described as if it were the elegant and smooth sine wave pictured in Figure 4. The gray section represents normal mood (described earlier in Chapter 3), while the vertical lines represent time in weeks, months or years.

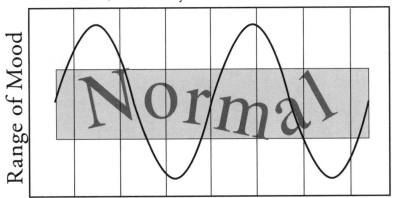

Range of Mood

Time in Weeks, Months or Years

Figure 4—Theory

Picturing your moods as a "sine wave" may make you think your moods swing in an even arch that follows the same path repeatedly. In this picture, your mood gradually cycles through mania, then slowly turns the corner and ebbs down through normal to depression and back again. Is this how you visualize bipolar disorder?

Most people with bipolar disorder wish this image was their reality; it actually applies for a very few people. Indeed, experiencing such a gentle course of ups and downs would at least allow you to know what to expect from time to time and brace for a change.

In reality, the image of bipolar disorder more closely resembles the diagram in Figure 5 rather than the smooth sine wave shown in Figure 4. The stars show the moods of a person experiencing bipolar disorder as erratic and unstable. Indeed, the number of times you pass through "normal" can be scarce or even absent. That is why it may be difficult for those who experience bipolar disorder to imagine normal mood. As you slowly move from mania to depression, you may not recognize

Time in Weeks, Months or Years
Figure 5—Reality

when your mood falls into the normal range. It is more likely you would awaken to experience a mood that has changed without warning overnight. This sudden change sometimes causes you to feel as though you don't really know who you are at any given time; your moods change without warning.

THE CONCEPT OF PLACE

Besides recognizing sudden mood swings, you need to know this further insight. When you experience mania, your previous experience of depression seems as if it never happened. Likewise, while experiencing depression, it is difficult to imagine feeling anything like mania. It's as though you are in a "place" rather than in a mood. Yet, you do travel from place to place—sometimes at lightning speed—when your mood changes. Many people with bipolar disorder use the concept of place to answer the inevitable question, "How are you today?" Instead of going through a litany of difficulties, they simply say, "I'm not in a very good place right now." This lets the person experiencing difficulty avoid painful explanations while allowing concerned individuals to be sensitive.

This feature of mood change is important to understand because you'll have additional insight into bipolar illness. Be aware that you may not recognize the other side of the bipolar coin when experiencing either mania or depression. Knowing that an extreme experience of mania can lead to a deeper depression helps you set goals outside of your immediate mood. These goals might include staying in treatment, even if you feel well, and pacing yourself to better manage your symptoms. (This chapter later looks at mood charting for managing symptoms.)

TYPES OF MOODS

Mixed mood

Let's look at the occurrence of a type of mood that can be confusing. In Figure 5, the stars may occupy the areas of mania and depression at the same time. This "mixed mood" implies that symptoms of both mania and depression occur simultaneously. These might include the irritability, increased energy and sleep loss of mania, plus the feelings of hopelessness and lack of enjoyment of depression.

Do you remember learning that the term bipolar is misleading because it implies two opposite and mutually exclusive moods? Remember, the core of the disorder is the brain's inability to consistently regulate mood within a normal range. Consequently, if regulation of mood cannot occur normally, then your mood can be all over the place—a mixed mood.

Rapid cycling

Whenever I use the term "rapid cycling," my husband says he doesn't think I'm riding my bicycle especially fast! However, in reference to bipolar disorder, rapid cycling refers to experiencing mood switches between mania and depression within a short period. Officially, rapid cycling is defined as switching back and forth from mania to depression four or more times in one year. Rapid cycling often occurs more frequently than this, even on a daily or hourly basis. This can be especially frustrating to the person experiencing it because it's extremely hard to hold on to a sense of self when one's mood changes rapidly.

Mood Charts for Symptoms

You might benefit from creating mood charts to better understand changes in your mood and to better manage your symptoms. You can do this by using a scale like the one shown in Figure 6.

In this scale, zero represents normal mood, minus five represents suicidal depression, and plus five stands for extreme mania requiring hospitalization. To keep a mood chart, put an X or dot on the number that represents your mood at a given time and do this once or twice a day. Do not be overly concerned about being exactly correct when identifying your mood. The idea is not to have a perfect mood chart but to become more aware of moods and how they change. For example, you may find it easy to recognize depression, but it's also easy to

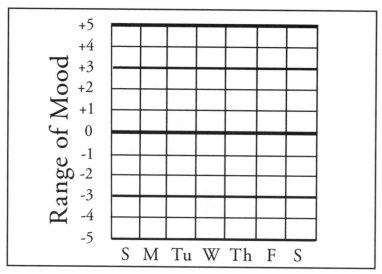

Figure 6—Plus/Minus Mood Chart

overstate its intensity. For most, mania is more difficult to recognize and its level is easy to understate. When you experience mixed mood or rapid cycling, put more than one X or dot for a given time or day.

Advantages of a mood chart

Consider these advantages of keeping a mood chart:

1. It helps you identify moods and their intensity. This will seem difficult at first but learning about mood and its changes from depression to mania can help you gain insights into your illness.

2. Second, it's an excellent tool for use in treatment because it helps you give an accurate description of your illness to doctors and therapists. This allows them to understand whether treatment is effective or whether changes need to be made.

3. Keeping a mood chart can help you manage your illness. When you see your mood rising toward mania, you can slow yourself down by breathing deeply or by doing an activity such as walking. It helps you regulate the high energy you are feeling. Reaching a high level on the mood chart may be the trigger needed to call your doctor or therapist for an appointment. When your mood chart shows depression, you can manage by planning fewer activities. You can call a friend or go

for a bike ride. You can call your doctor or therapist if the depression continues in a downward direction, especially if you feel like you could harm yourself or others. Many people record their medications and dosages on their mood charts. This can help you and your doctor monitor your medications. It can also remind you to take your medications as they are prescribed.

4. A mood chart can help you see the relationship between depression and mania, and be realistic about your illness. Clearly, seeing the relationship between depression and mania can help you manage symptoms. The goal is not necessarily to reach "normal" mood but to have a narrower range of mood and avoid the extremes.

SUMMARY

Treatment for bipolar disorder does not aim to change your personality, but rather to spare you the extremes and rapid shifts of mood that make it difficult to express your special gifts.

In looking at the moods of bipolar disorder, recognize that at the core is your brain's inability to consistently regulate mood within a normal range. Mood is certainly more than feeling happy or sad; it affects the very core of your being. Regulation of mood is an issue that most people do not need to face every day. But it is a challenge to all who experience the extreme or unpredictable moods of bipolar disorder.

How can you meet this challenge? By actively participating

in treatment and developing management skills for symptoms of the illness. Many have developed these skills and their numbers are growing daily. Find out more about these management skills by reading books and articles, joining a recovery-focused group and using community resources.

You want to recover from bipolar disorder. The next three chapters address the recovery process.

Recovering from Bipolar Disorder

THE CORE concept of this book is that insight is the first step to recovery. But what exactly does recovery mean in the context of bipolar disorder?

There could be as many definitions of recovery from bipolar disorder as there are people who have the disorder. One narrow definition of recovery is "a person has no more symptoms and no longer needs treatment." However, this definition doesn't square with the facts that bipolar disorder tends to be a chronic illness with recurring episodes. Others define recovery more realistically to allow for treatment of symptoms that will always be a part of your life.

Most, however, agree that recovery in the context of bipolar disorder is an ongoing process that implies movement, change and growth. The movement involves an ebb and flow of symptoms, not a steady change in one direction. That's why periods of discouragement as well as periods of hope need to be accepted as part of the process. A tree not only grows upward toward the sun; it also grows in twists and knots. Pruning away branches encourages new and healthy growth. The results are seen in the harvest that arrives months or years later.

A process has a clear vision for a place where you want to be. Growth recognizes a give and take in movement forward and backward, even though the overall direction is toward specific goals.

ACTIVELY PURSUE WELLNESS

My working definition of recovery is: *Recovery is a process in which an individual actively pursues mental wellness in the context of experiencing a neurobiologic disorder.*

You are likely aware, as I often am, that *recovery* can be a painful word. When we experience severe depression or discouragement in meeting goals because of mania, the word *recovery* has an impossible ring to it.

Still, if recovery seems unachievable right now, I ask you to push aside the word "impossible." Do not think of recovery in absolute terms that discourage you from pursuing it. Instead, look upon it as a journey that will take you through frustration and joy.

To begin recovery, look at where you are and where you've been. Do your venting and grieving, but don't stop with that. If you have regrets, remember, you've always done the best you could. You may be capable of doing better now or in the future, but to recover, you need to accept the past and present in the context of your experience with bipolar disorder.

Adopting this philosophy is difficult, but if you are willing, you can learn how to grow tall like the tree—even in the face of the shifting winds of mood changes.

Recovery means moving toward the productive and satisfying life you choose. You may begin by making leaps and bounds toward the life you want, but more likely recovery takes the form of two steps forward and one step back. You measure progress in inches on some days, and in miles on other days.

MY OWN JOURNEY

In my own life, I have seen many people who were very ill from bipolar disorder gain their independence, return to work and carve out a happy social life. I saw how they made varying degrees of progress at different times. In most cases, their lives changed greatly while they were developing career goals, building social circles in which they now move and pacing the events in their lives.

When I was extremely ill with depression, I had a deep conviction that I would either kill myself or I would recover over many years. Many times, I came close to ending my journey because recovery was coming so slowly.

But however slow, recovery is possible. I still experience symptoms that make for challenging days and even months. Yet overall my direction is toward a meaningful life. I started this journey by taking baby steps—and promptly fell down.

As a parent, I remember a special day in our son's life (even though he has no memory of his amazing feat). Our son learned to crawl early at five months. Then, for seven months, he cruised around the house, mostly crawling. Then one day, he watched a younger neighbor girl walk all over our living room, exploring everything in sight. My husband and I could even see him thinking as we watched. To our surprise, he took his first four tiny steps before falling down and returning to his usual crawl.

As parents, our son could have done nothing else to elicit more joy. It was a delight! We saw him in the context of the moment, taking baby steps and then falling. Neither of us said, "He should be running by now," or, "How come he isn't playing in Little League?" or, "How come he hasn't graduated from high school?" Instead, we rejoiced and praised him for his momentous achievement. It did not matter that we didn't see him walk again the next day; we were every bit as thrilled at his next four steps two days later.

REJOICE WITH EVERY STEP

When you consider recovery, become your own best parent and rejoice in your first baby steps. Do not be discouraged by others who may not be able to see these baby steps as accomplishments. If you are experiencing depression and feel immobilized, your first baby step may be to get out of bed and take a shower. That may be all that you can do that day, but because it is moving forward, it is as great an accomplishment as my son's first steps. Next, you may be able to attend a recovery group with a friend.

If you are experiencing mania, your baby step may be stopping for a few seconds and slowing down your thoughts as you take deep breaths from the pit of your stomach. No matter where you are on your journey, remember my son taking his first steps. Look at someone else taking baby steps, someone focused on making a daily habit of trying on the habit of recovery. Once you start looking, you will find many others who take this approach. Ask them how they do it, rejoice in their successes and share your own with them.

Finding Support for Recovery

YOU ARE committed to recovery. Now, how do you find the support you need? Do such groups even exist? How do you contact them?

You might believe that you don't know of any recovery groups or even any others who have bipolar disorder. This simply can't be true. Depending on the source of the statistics, up to 2% of the population in the USA has bipolar disorder— that's over five million people!

So if you know 100 people, it is likely you know at least one other person who has bipolar disorder.

DISCLOSURE

Unfortunately, you probably do not know who that other person is, nor does that person know you have bipolar disorder. This brings up the issue of disclosure, telling others that you have bipolar disorder. Because of discrimination and fear of being rejected, many people who experience bipolar disorder do not want to tell others about it. Clinicians carefully guard their client's identities to protect them from discrimination.

Good reasons to keep your diagnosis a secret include financial and emotional ones. You might be afraid of job discrimination. You may feel a sense of shame about your illness. You may have faced rejection from close friends and relatives when they learned of your diagnosis. You may fear losing your health, disability or life insurance coverage if you disclose your diagnosis.

You may choose to disclose your diagnosis to a few close friends or tell nearly everyone. I have chosen to do the latter. For me, this has been a safe decision because I'm self-employed and working actively in mental health advocacy as a professional speaker, consultant and author. However, I have friends who have lost their jobs because they told someone at work they experience bipolar disorder.

The risks of losing job, family, friends or financial security are real. But there are also potential benefits to disclosing your disorder. For example, you no longer have to hide or feel ashamed and can develop supportive relationships with others who experience bipolar disorder. Sad to say, disclosure may also reveal who your true friends are.

Most of all, you gain the ability to educate others about the special challenges you face. Doing this, you often get essential support you might not have had otherwise.

Yet no matter what you decide about disclosure, it is healthy to develop and maintain friendships both with people who experience bipolar disorder and with those who do not. This gives you a balance that allows you to have a frame of reference both "with" and "beyond" your illness. It helps you gain the understanding and support you need for recovery and helps you get outside of your disorder.

LEGAL PROTECTION

If you choose to disclose to an employer, consider getting help in doing this from a Disabilities Specialist, especially if there are performance issues involved that could lead to your being fired. You also may have certain legal protections from the Americans with Disabilities Act or the Federal Rehabilitation Act of 1973 and its subsequent revisions.

A PERSON WITH TALENTS

Remember, you are an individual with bipolar disorder just as you are an individual with music or art talent or the ability to do mathematics or sew or work on cars. You also are a person with relationships that need to be nurtured. This is the goal of recovery—that you remain an individual with interests and activities that you find rewarding and relationships that you find meaningful. If your illness has derailed your sense of self, take it as a challenge to get back on track.

CHOOSE SUPPORT WISELY

You may choose to have only a few close friends or family know about your experiences. When you share with others, explain that what you are sharing about bipolar disorder is private. Choose your confidants wisely. Similarly, select a recovery group in which confidentiality is taught and observed. If you are uncertain about visiting a certain group, call the group leader and ask about confidentiality within the group.

Guidance on Using Respectful Language

Have you ever thought about how the language you use affects the way you feel about yourself?

When you were in sports and on the second string, did you ever say something like, "I'm just on the second string." The word "just" in this sentence conveys the message that second string is a lesser position than first string. Qualifiers (like the word "just" in the example above) express how we feel about ourselves while communicating specific impressions that may not be respectful. Indeed, we send out messages of self-respect or poor self-esteem through our choice of words.

For example, remembering names may be difficult for you. If you frequently tell yourself and others that you can't remember names, you reinforce your belief that the problem exists. In reality, nearly everyone has to work to remember names of others.

Another example relates to how you may have viewed yourself as a child. Maybe you said, "I'm just a kid" instead of saying, "I am a person who is growing, learning and influencing my world." These two statements feel quite different to both the speaker and the listener.

Likewise, the language you use to refer to mental disorders can also influence the way you feel about yourself. When you received a diagnosis of having bipolar disorder for the first time, you probably heard language that changed how you viewed yourself. The first thing your doctor or therapist said may have sounded something like this: "You're bipolar," meaning you have a diagnosis of bipolar disorder. Others may have referred to you as "a bipolar" or a "bipolar person." You may even think of yourself in this way. This way of speaking implies (to yourself and others) that you **are** your illness.

Interestingly, we don't do this with most other disorders, although we do refer to "diabetics" or "asthmatics" and "alcoholics." But we would never refer to someone with cancer as being "cancerous" or call him "a cancer." Yet with mental disorders, it is commonly accepted to call an individual a "bipolar" or a "schizophrenic." I believe we deserve to be identified as people, not as disorders.

Many mental health advocates have adopted what is called person-first language. This means we always put the person before the diagnosis. Thus, we'd say, "I am a person who has bipolar disorder" or "I am a person who experiences the symptoms of bipolar disorder."

Remember, each one of us is far more than our diagnosis. I am a wife, a mother, a physician, a violinist and a member of Toastmasters. I take pride in all of these roles that define me. But you can raise my ire by calling me "a bipolar" because I do not define myself in this way. This doesn't mean that I will not talk about having bipolar disorder and the challenges it creates. But when I speak about myself, I want to use words that convey respect and growth in self-esteem. I do not want to be my illness, even though that illness plays a significant role in my life.

I encourage you to use person-first language for at least a month and see how it makes you feel about yourself. If you are comfortable with it, begin to educate others. To do this, communicate with directness. When another person speaks of "a bipolar" and you respond with "do you mean a person who has bipolar disorder?" it does not get the idea across well enough. You want people to change their language, thus change their perspective toward those who *have bipolar disorder. So be direct and say, "I prefer that we speak of people as individuals rather than as diagnoses. Do you mind saying a person with bipolar disorder rather than 'a bipolar'?" That approach would be more effective and more memorable.*

Use these examples of respectful language—

- *"My brother experiences bipolar disorder" rather than "My brother is bipolar."*
- *"I have bipolar disorder" rather than "I am bipolar."*
- *"I am a doctor and I also have bipolar disorder" but not "I'm a bipolar doctor."*
- *"The symptoms of bipolar disorder affect my life" but not "Because I'm bipolar, I sometimes have trouble concentrating."*
- *"I need to miss work today because I am ill" but not "I'm bipolar so I can't go to work today."*
- *"Many people in my family are challenged by bipolar disorder" but not "We have bipolars all through our family tree."*

When you respect yourself in your use of language, you will be respected in return!

Making Recovery Groups Work

I T IS IMPORTANT to understand that recovery groups do not provide therapy. Professionals don't usually lead them unless they themselves also have bipolar disorder. Rather than providing treatment, they are a source of support from others who share the common experience of bipolar disorder.

In addition, recovery groups should encourage you to be in treatment or be actively seeking treatment. They should also provide education to help you gain crucial insight, plus give you an opportunity to share and learn from others.

A recovery group should respect your confidentiality and have a policy to ensure confidentiality. You may consider many aspects of your experience to be private; you clearly don't want other group members to "tell the world" about them.

Your support group should be comfortable enough for you to vent your frustrations, yet focused enough to encourage you to take positive steps toward recovery. Its emphasis should be on encouragement and active problem solving. An important question that group members might ask each other is, "What are you doing to take care of yourself?" Perhaps this question should provide the foundation for any discussion.

SEEKING A GROUP

To find a recovery group, call these organizations: National Mental Health Association, National Alliance for the Mentally Ill (NAMI), Depression and Bipolar Support Alliance (formerly Depressive and Manic-Depressive Association) or The United Way. Ask them to search their computer banks for bipolar recovery groups in your area. Often, recovery groups are not specific to those who have bipolar disorder but serve people who experience either depression or bipolar disorder. If you don't find a group exclusively for individuals with bipolar disorder, ask about depression recovery groups or support groups that are for people with depression and bipolar disorder. Also ask for a list of Clubhouses or Drop-in Centers you can attend.

Clubhouses are organizations that provide occupational services, support and the development of a recovery model for individuals with neurobiologic disorders. They are certified by the International Clubhouse Association. Drop-in Centers are usually run by peers, and they therefore provide an opportunity to be with others facing similar challenges. Programming is determined by the group's focus and may include educational opportunities, recovery groups and social activities. These facilities offer programs that can empower you to move on with your life. You can also contact local Community Mental Health Centers.

When you start to look for a group, take time to attend three or four meetings to get a picture of the group's emphasis. If it doesn't meet your needs, move on to another group. If moving on isn't possible, challenge the group leaders to make the focus of the group more helpful and more hopeful.

AA Groups

Many who have been unable to find a recovery group specific to bipolar disorder have joined Alcoholics Anonymous (AA), even though they don't have a problem with alcohol. Several of my friends have done this.

AA groups meet frequently and have the advantage of having chapters located nearly everywhere, even in remote communities. If you do not have a drinking problem, when people at the meeting say, "I am an alcoholic," instead you can say, "I experience bipolar disorder." If one AA group doesn't accept and support you, move on to another group.

Since as many as 60% of people with bipolar disorder also have addiction problems, you may easily meet others who have bipolar disorder. Together may want to start your own group specifically for those with bipolar disorder. Eventually you will see more recovery groups forming that are specifically intended for individuals with bipolar disorder. But for now, use every resource you can find.

Research shows that recovery most often occurs within a supportive community. In cultures and societies that need and accept individuals despite their illnesses, the recovery rate from neurobiologic disorders is much higher than in cultures where people with such disorders are hidden away or shunned.

When we don't readily find acceptance in our lives, we often turn to self-help or biographical books written about others who have experienced mental disorders. Reading about others and their experiences can increase your insight into bipolar disorder, but you will still benefit from being with others who share your challenges.

Start Your Own Group

When I couldn't find a group in my area to meet my needs, I started one myself. If you choose to do this, don't do it alone. You might plan a couple of meetings solo to get started, but consider carefully whether to continue if others are not willing to help. Be aware that starting a recovery group can greatly increase the stress in your life.

What worked for me was to line up speakers for a few meetings and hand out flyers to advertise their talks. If you can't locate a speaker, call community groups or get videotapes from groups such as the Mental Health Association, the National Alliance for the Mentally Ill or the Depression and Bipolar Support Alliance (formerly Depressive and Manic-Depressive Association). Hospitals or medical schools could be a source of speakers or provide help starting a group.

At the first meeting of the group I started, we took a break after the presentation and then held an organizational meeting attended by only five or six people who were all willing to be on the Steering Committee. A Steering Committee takes responsibility for planning future meetings. In our case, the Steering Committee devised a system for keeping track of attendance, arranging speakers and planning refreshments.

During the first two years, the Steering Committee planned a facilitator training and a birthday party. After several months, we quit promoting our groups since we were growing too rapidly to keep things manageable. Other community groups and clinicians began promoting our group without even being asked!

You can usually find a church or religious group to provide a free meeting space for your recovery group. If you are having trouble finding a location, ask The United Way for suggestions. (If you would like to attend a seminar on how to start a recovery group or on training for small group facilitators, see the Order Form at the end of this book.)

Other resources in your community include Mental Health Centers. You can also call your HMO or PPO to see whether they have such groups. Ask your doctor or therapist about recovery groups in your area. Another resource for finding groups is the psychiatry department at local hospitals. They often have lists of recovery groups to give to patients. Of course, many groups will have their own web sites.

CHAT ROOM SUPPORT QUESTIONABLE

If you have access to the Internet, you can search for information about recovery and recovery groups. You can even participate in chat rooms for people experiencing bipolar disorder. An alternative is Alcoholics Anonymous (AA), which has web sites for those who live in isolated areas or who cannot go to meetings because of disability.

I have found chat rooms helpful in a limited way. While being part of a chat room helped me feel less isolated when I was experiencing depression, it did not help me move forward in my life. Unfortunately, those with mania dominated. Most of the chat was simply far too rapid for me to join in. Also, you must be careful choosing a chat room if you are likely to reveal personal information. Confidentiality could be a problem because what you share online becomes public knowledge. You may receive more than spam if you reveal too much to the wrong people.

ONE STEP AT A TIME

Here are some ideas for getting started in a recovery group. It may be difficult for you to actually attend a group. But remember to be your own best parent and praise yourself for taking that first baby step toward recovery. If you find it difficult to get out or if you are afraid to visit a group, call the person in charge of the group. Many of the regular attendees of the group I founded called me before they dared to come to an actual meeting. Now they attend regularly. Learning in advance about the group and how it is run will also make you feel more comfortable the first time you attend. You're certain to know one other person in the group, even though you only met over the phone.

It may help to attend your first group with a friend or relative. Many groups welcome them and have separate small groups for friends and family while you attend your own. Look for a group that emphasizes recovery rather than encourages only venting. Venting in support groups is OK if you need to do that. But after a brief time of venting, a recovery-oriented group will encourage you to ask what you can do to take care of yourself. They will share their own experiences and focus on steps you can take to manage symptoms and challenges.

Conclusion—My Wish for You

D O YOU remember my definition of recovery? *Recovery is a process in which a person actively seeks mental wellness in the context of experiencing a neurobiologic disorder.* This book began with the desire to foster hope for you and those close to you. My goal remains to help you expand and nourish that hope in your life.

I believe that insight is the first step to hope and recovery. My wish for you is that you gain the insight you need to begin and continue your own recovery process. You can develop that insight by learning about bipolar disorder and by incorporating nurturing support in your own recovery. Recovery happens when you obtain treatment, but also with support from your friends and family and the community where you live.

May your journey on this educational path expand and enrich your world as you seek mental wellness for yourself and others.

Glossary

Glossary

Addiction disorder—A disorder characterized by physical or psychological dependence on a substance.

Anhedonia—A symptom of depression in which a person lacks enjoyment of things that normally would be enjoyable. From words meaning *without pleasure.*

Bipolar disorder—A mood disorder in which the brain does not consistently regulate mood within a normal range. Bipolar disorder includes a spectrum of disorders. (See Bipolar I disorder, Bipolar II disorder and Cyclothymic disorder.) From words meaning *two poles.*

Bipolar I—A bipolar disorder whose chief characteristic is mania punctuated by depression.

Bipolar II—A bipolar disorder whose chief characteristic is depression punctuated by hypomania.

Blue mood—A mood within the normal range of mood that is characterized by feeling sad but doesn't have sufficient intensity or duration to be described as depression.

Brain disorder—A neurobiologic or mental disorder. This term is sometimes used to define a narrow group of disorders that have been proven scientifically to have a biological basis.

Clubhouse—An organization that provides occupational services, support and the development of a recovery model for individuals with neurobiologic disorders.

Cognitive—Having to do with thinking.

Comorbidity—The existence of more than one disorder, disease or illness at the same time in the same person.

Concentration—The act of directing of one's thoughts to one topic to the exclusion of other topics.

Confidentiality—The practice of maintaining trust between two or more people by agreeing not to share information to third parties without permission. From words meaning *with* and *to trust.*

Cycling—As it refers to bipolar disorder, the spontaneous change from one mood to another, as from hypomania to depression.

Cyclothymic disorder—A type of bipolar disorder that is characterized by mood changes with symptoms of mania and depression. Symptoms do not meet the full criteria for Major Depression or Hypomania, either because they are fewer than the required number or their duration is shorter than required.

Delusion—A false or mistaken belief. In bipolar disorder delusional thinking may have a biological basis, being associated with episodes of depression, mania, hypomania or mixed moods.

Depression—An episode of mood in which sadness and other typical symptoms such as loss of interest or pleasure last for at least two weeks and are intense enough to cause significant distress or impairment.

Disclosure—The act of telling facts to others about oneself or one's personal condition. In the context of bipolar disorder, disclosure is telling others of your diagnosis and experience of illness.

Drop-in center—A center run by peers that provides social services for its constituents such as classes and recovery groups.

Dual diagnoses—Having two diagnoses. In the context of bipolar disorder, the term dual diagnoses is often used to describe having bipolar disorder and a substance abuse or addiction disorder.

Dysphoria—A feeling of discomfort and unpleasantness. From a word meaning *excessive anguish.*

Elation—A feeling of great joy. Elation is within the range of normal mood rather than that of hypomania or mania because other symptoms do no accompany it, nor does it last for a full week.

Euphoria—A feeling of well-being or high spirits. With regard to bipolar disorder, euphoria is an exaggerated feeling of joy and pleasure that is beyond normal mood.

Grandiose thinking—In the context of bipolar disorder, grandiose thinking is a believing that one is capable of being greater than circumstances would support or of accomplishing more than is humanly possible.

Hallucination—A perception of seeing, hearing or smelling things which are not actually present. In bipolar disorder, hallucinations can be associated with either depression or mania/hypomania. Hallucinations are neurobiologic in origin.

Hypersomnia—Sleeping for longer periods than is normal. From words meaning *excessive* and *sleep*.

Hypomania—An episode of mood that is in a range above that of normal mood but that is not as extreme as mania. From words meaning *under* and *mania*.

Hyposomnia—Sleeping for shorter periods than is normal. In depression, hyposomnia is accompanied by fatigue. In mania or hypomania, hyposomnia is accompanied by increased energy level. From words meaning *under* and *sleep*.

Irritability—The condition of responding to annoyance in a way that is increased from normal. In bipolar disorder, irritability results in a low toleration for frustration. Irritability is different from anger in that it is diffusely directed at multiple annoyances rather at a particular target.

Mania—An episode of mood that is characterized by instability and that is above the range of normal mood.

Manic-depressive disorder—An older term that is still often used for bipolar disorder.

Mental disorder—A disorder that results from an abnormality in the structure, chemistry or physiology of the brain.

Mental health provider—A healthcare worker who provides clinical services that lead to better mental health or that treat neurobiologic disorders. Mental health providers include clinicians from a wide range of disciplines, namely, counselors, psychiatric nurse practitioners, psychiatrists, psychologists, social workers and therapists. Mental health provider in some instances also refers to insurances or organizations that provide mental health services.

Mixed mood—An episode of mood outside the range of normal that includes symptoms of depression and mania/hypomania occurring at the same time.

Mood—Mood describes the prevailing emotions, thoughts and behaviors that reflect a person's state of mind or feeling. With regard to bipolar disorder, there are five basic moods: normal, depression, hypomania, mania and mixed mood. From words meaning *mind, soul, courage, mental disposition, spirit, custom.*

Mood chart—A written chart that is used to rate the level of mood that a person is experiencing from the extreme of suicidal depression to normal to extreme mania.

Neurobiologic disorder—A disorder that has its origin in the structure or physiology of the brain. From words meaning *nerve* and *life.*

Normal mood—Mood that is regulated by the brain to stay within a normal range. Normal mood varies and includes sadness and elation but underlying normal mood is a feeling of contentment or happiness most of the time.

Peer—A person of equal rank. In reference to bipolar disorder, a peer is another individual who also has bipolar disorder. From a word meaning *equal.*

Person first language—Language respectful of the person being talked about by recognizing the person rather than equating the person with a disorder or condition. Example: "I experience symptoms of bipolar disorder," rather than "I am bipolar."

Pressure of speech—A condition usually associated with mania or hypomania, in which there is a strong propensity to keep talking. Speech may be rapid and "conversations" may be one-sided with the speaker finding it difficult to stop speaking long enough to listen to the other person.

Psychomotor agitation—A condition often associated with mania, in which increased physical motion is associated with increased mental activity.

Psychomotor retardation—A condition often associated with depression, in which decreased physical activity is associated with a slowing of mental activity.

Psychosis—A condition in which there is a break from reality or one's personality.

Psychotherapy—Treatment whose goal is improved mental health. In the context of bipolar disorder, many effective psychotherapy treatments have been developed which result in fewer hospitalizations and extremes of mood. Psychotherapy is sometimes called "talk therapy." From two words meaning *mind* and *treatment*.

Racing thoughts—Rapid thinking associated with mania or hypomania. Often the person experiencing racing thoughts will not perceive them as such but will have the sensation that the world has slowed down or that thoughts are intrusive, interfering with concentration and focus.

Rapid cycling—Technically, rapid cycling is diagnosed when there are four or more distinct episodes of depression, mania or hypomania within one year. However, the episodes are likely to be more frequent than four times yearly.

Recovery—A process in which a person actively seeks mental wellness in the context of experiencing a neurobiologic disorder.

Recovery groups—In reference to bipolar disorder, individuals with bipolar disorder and concerned friends or family who meet regularly with goals of education, mutual support and sharing of skills for living well with bipolar disorder.

Self-medicating—A term used to refer to the act of dampening emotional or physical pain by using a substance of abuse such as alcohol or street drugs. This term is not particularly accurate and it fails to recognize the co-occurrence of mental disorders with addictive disorders.

Substance abuse disorder—A pattern of substance use that results in repeated and significant negative consequences due to the use of that substance.

Syndrome—A group of symptoms reported by individuals and signs observed by others that together form a recognizable pattern of disease or disorder. From words meaning *together* and *running.*

Therapy—Any treatment for an illness or disorder. From a word meaning *treatment.*

Triggers—Situations or activities that lead to an increase of symptoms.

Unipolar depression—A pattern of depression in which depression and normal mood are the only moods that exist over time. Unipolar depression is distinguished from bipolar depression in that episodes of mania, hypomania or mixed mood are not present at any time. Unipolar is made of up two words meaning *one* and *pole.*

Recovery Resources

Books

Berger, Diane and Berger, Lisa. *We Heard the Angels of Madness: A Family Guide to Coping with Manic Depression.* Quill William Morrow, 1991.

Burns, David. *Feeling Good Handbook.* Plume, 1999.

Burns, David and Beck, Aaron T. *Feeling Good: The New Mood Therapy.* Avon, 1999.

Copeland, Mary Ellen. *Living without Depression & Manic Depression: A Workbook for Maintaining Mood Stability.* New Harbinger Publications, Inc., 1994.

Copeland, Mary Ellen. *Wellness Recovery Action Plan.* Peach Press, 1997, revised 2000.

Copeland, Mary Ellen. *Winning Against Relapse: A Workbook of Action Plans for Recurring Health and Emotional Problem.* New Harbinger Publications, Inc., 1999.

Duke, Patty and Pinckert, Mary Lou and Hochman, Gloria. *A Brilliant Madness: Living With Manic-Depressive Illness.* Bantam, 1993.

Duke, Patty and Turan, Kenneth. *Call Me Anna: The Autobiography of Patty Duke*. Bantam, 1990.

Fieve, Ronald R. *Moodswing: Dr. Fieve on Depression (revised edition)*. Bantam Books, 1997.

Mental Health: A Report of the Surgeon General. United States Government Printing Office, 1999.

Miklowitz, David J. *The Bipolar Disorder Survival Guide: What You and Your Family Need to Know*. The Guilford Press, 2002.

Mondimore, Francis Mark. *Bipolar Disorder: A Guide for Patients and Families*. The Johns Hopkins University Press, 1999.

Newman, Cory F. and Leahy, Robert L. and Beck, Aaron T. and Reilly-Harrington and Noreen A. *Bipolar Disorder: A Cognitive Therapy Approach*. American Psychological Association, 2002.

Quinnett, Paul. *Suicide: the Forever Decision, for Those Thinking About Suicide and Those Who Know, Love and Counsel Them*. Free PDF download: www.qprinstitute.com.

Ramirez Basco, Monica and Rush, A. John. *Cognitive-Behavioral Therapy for Bipolar Disorder*. The Guilford Press, 1996.

Redfield Jamison, Kay. *Night Falls Fast: Understanding Suicide*. Vintage Books, 2000.

Redfield Jamison, Kay. *An Unquiet Mind*. Random House, 1997.

Redfield Jamison. *Touched with Fire: Manic-Depressive Illness and the Artistic Temperament*. Free Press, 1996.

Waltz, Mitzi. *Bipolar Disorders: A Guide to Helping Children & Adolescents*. Patient-Centered Guides, 2000.

Organizations

Al-Anon and Alateen. www.al-anon.alateen.org

Alcoholics Anonymous. www.alcoholicsanonymous.org

Depression and Bipolar Support Alliance, 730 N. Franklin Street, Suite 501, Chicago, IL 60610-7204. 1.800.826.3632, 312.642.0049. www.ndmda.org

Canadian Mental Health Association. www.cmha.ca

County Mental Health Centers

Double Trouble in Recovery. www.gotomytown.com/rog/ NonProfits/doubletrouble.htm

Empower Colorado. www.empowercolorado.com

Federation of Families for Children's Mental Health, 1101 King Street, Suite 420 Alexandria, VA 22314. www.ffcmh.org/ Eng_one.htm

National Alliance for the Mentally Ill. Colonial Place Three, 2107 Wilson Blvd., Suite 300, Arlington, VA 22201. 1.800.950.6264. www.nami.org

National Institutes of Mental Health (NIMH), Biological Psychiatry Branch, Building 10, Room 3N212, 9000 Rockville Pike, Bethesda, MD 20892. www.nih.gov

National Mental Health Association, 1021 Prince Street, Aexandria, VA 22314-2971. 1.800.969.6642, www.nmha.org

QPR Insititute. P.O. Box 2867, Spokane, WA 99220. 1.888.726.7926, www.qprinsitute.com

United Way. www.unitedway.org

Yellow Ribbon Suicide Prevention Program: Light for Life Foundation International. www.yellowribbon.org

Wellness Recovery Action Plan (WRAP). www.copeland@mental healthrecovery.com, or www.marellencopeland.com

Quick Order Form

Chapter One Press
Box 300039
Denver, CO 80203-0039

Name:

Address:

City:

State: Zip:

Telephone:

Email address:

_____ books @ $19.95 each =   _____

Sales tax: 7.2% for book(s)
   shipped to a Colorado address =   _____

Shipping and handling: $5.00 per book (up to a maximum of
$20.00) =   _____

Total: _____

Please send FREE information:

❏   How can I attend future seminars and workshops by
      Dr. Mountain?

❏   How can I arrange to have Dr. Mountain speak at my
      group or meeting?

Please send your order via check or money order payable to
Chapter One Press

Visit our website to order online:
www.beyondbipolar.com